Collins

AQA GCSE

Biology

Higher

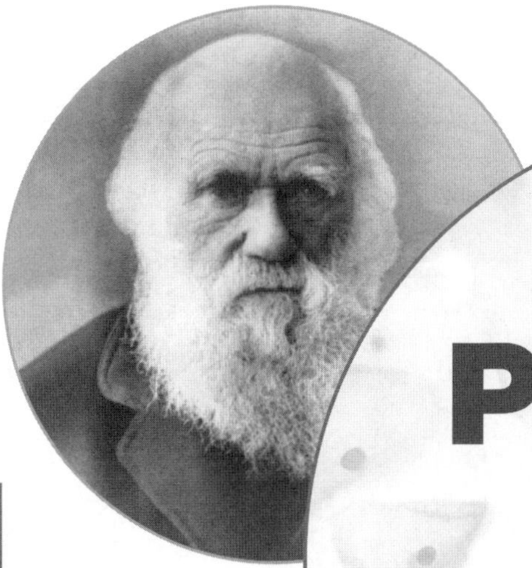

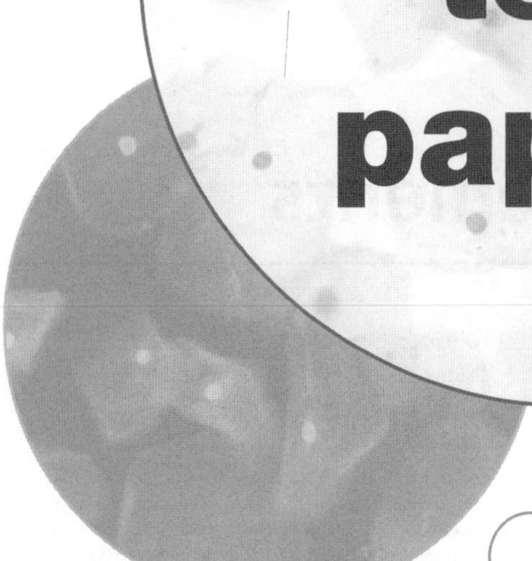

Practice test papers

Mike Smith and Kath Skillern

Biology

Higher

AQA GCSE 9-1

Practice test papers

2 x tests

Contents

SET A

Paper 1 3

Paper 2 23

SET B

Paper 1 47

Paper 2 63

ANSWERS 87

Acknowledgements

The authors and publisher are grateful to the copyright holders for permission to use quoted materials and images.
All images are © HarperCollins*Publishers* and Shutterstock.com
Every effort has been made to trace copyright holders and obtain their permission for the use of copyright material. The author and publisher will gladly receive information enabling them to rectify any error or omission in subsequent editions. All facts are correct at time of going to press.
Published by Collins
An imprint of HarperCollins*Publishers*
1 London Bridge Street
London SE1 9GF

© HarperCollins*Publishers* Limited 2019
ISBN 9780008321413
First published 2019
10 9 8 7 6 5 4 3 2 1
All rights reserved. No part of this publication may be reproduced, stored in a retrieval system, or transmitted, in any form or by any means, electronic, mechanical, photocopying, recording or otherwise, without the prior permission of Collins.
British Library Cataloguing in Publication Data.
A CIP record of this book is available from the British Library.

Commissioning Editor: Kerry Ferguson
Project Leader and Management: Chantal Addy and Shelley Teasdale
Authors: Mike Smith and Kath Skillern
Cover Design: Sarah Duxbury
Inside Concept Design: Ian Wrigley
Text Design and Layout: QBS Learning
Production: Karen Nulty
Printed in Martins the Printers Ltd

Collins

AQA
GCSE
Biology
SET A – Paper 1 Higher Tier

H

Author: Mike Smith

Materials

Time allowed: 1 hour 45 minutes

For this paper you must have:
- a ruler
- a calculator.

Instructions

- Answer **all** questions in the spaces provided.
- Do all rough work in this book. Cross through any work you do not want to be marked.

Information

- There are 100 marks available on this paper.
- The marks for questions are shown in brackets.
- You are expected to use a calculator where appropriate.
- You are reminded of the need for good English and clear presentation in your answers.
- When answering questions 03.1, 09.2 and 10.2 you need to make sure that your answer:
  – is clear, logical, sensibly structured
  – fully meets the requirements of the question
  – shows that each separate point or step supports the overall answer.

Advice

- In all calculations, show clearly how you work out your answer.

Name:

01 The human body protects itself against pathogens in different ways.

01.1 Draw **one** line from each part of the body to the way it protects the body against pathogens.

Part of the body	Way it protects the body
Platelets	Acts as a barrier
Skin	Forms clots to seal wounds
Stomach	Secretes mucus to trap pathogens
Trachea and bronchi	Produces acid to kill pathogens

[3 marks]

01.2 Describe **one** advantage and **one** disadvantage of using antibiotics against pathogens.

Advantage: _____

Disadvantage: _____

[2 marks]

01.3 Explain how vaccination can protect the body against illness caused by pathogens.

_____

_____

_____

_____

[4 marks]

02 Many organisms are multicellular.

02.1 Figure 2.1 shows an image of a white blood cell.

Figure 2.1

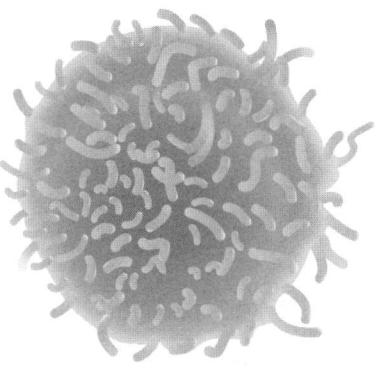

The diameter of the image is 60 mm

The image has been magnified 5000 times.

Calculate the actual size of the cell in μm

Use the formula:

$$\text{magnification} = \frac{\text{size of image}}{\text{size of real object}}$$

Actual size: .... μm   **[4 marks]**

Question 2 continues on the next page

02.2 Electron microscopes can be used to view sub-cellular structures in detail.

Electron microscopes have a greater resolution (resolving power) than light microscopes.

Explain the difference between **resolution** and **magnification**.

....

....

....

....
[2 marks]

02.3 **Figure 2.2** shows a single-celled organism called *Euglena*.

Figure 2.2

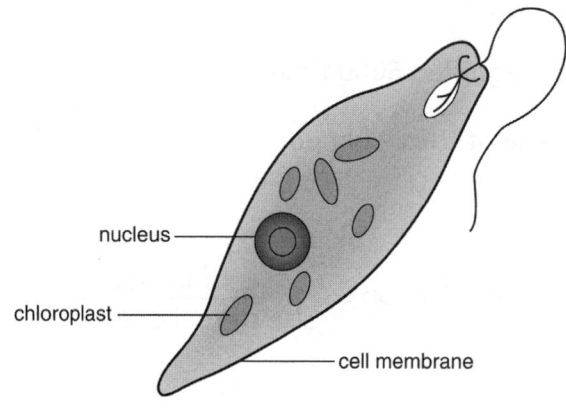

Euglena has been classified as a protist.

Suggest why it has **not** been classified as an animal, a plant or a bacterium.

It is **not** an animal because ....

....

It is **not** a plant because ....

....

It is **not** a bacterium because ....

....
[3 marks]

03 Amylase is an enzyme that digests starch to sugar.

The following method can be used to investigate the effect of pH on the activity of amylase.

1. Mix amylase solution and starch suspension in a boiling tube.
2. Put the boiling tube into a water bath at 25 °C
3. Remove a drop of the mixture every 30 seconds and test it for the presence of starch.
4. Repeat the investigation at different pH values.

03.1 The activity of amylase is also affected by temperature.

Use the method above to describe how you would investigate this. In your method, explain how you would identify the optimum temperature for amylase activity.

You should include:

- what you would measure
- variables you would control.

[6 marks]

Question 3 continues on the next page

03.2 Complete **Table 3.1**

Table 3.1

Enzyme	Substrate	Product
Amylase	Starch	Sugar
Protease		
Lipase		

[4 marks]

03.3 Describe how to test for sugars.

....

....

.... [3 marks]

04 A student grew some bacterial colonies from a pure culture on an agar plate.

Figure 4.1 shows the results.

Figure 4.1

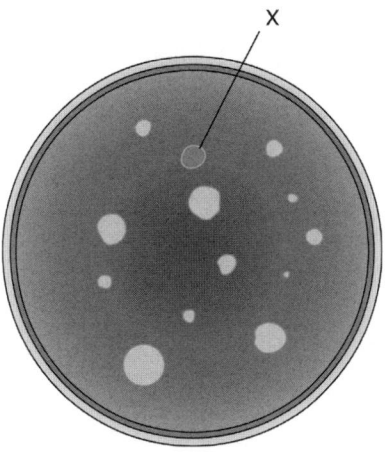

04.1 How many bacteria were originally put on the agar plate?

Give a reason for your answer.

How many: _____

Reason: _____

_____

[2 marks]

04.2 All the colonies look similar except for colony **X**.

Suggest why colony **X** looks different.

_____

_____

[1 mark]

Question 4 continues on the next page

04.3 Describe **two** ways the student could improve the practical technique to make sure all the colonies look similar.

1. ....

   ....

2. ....

   .... **[2 marks]**

04.4 The student measured the diameter of the largest colony as 17.0 mm

Calculate the cross-sectional area of the colony using the equation:

$$area = \pi r^2$$

Use $\pi = 3.14$

Give your answer in **mm² in standard form**.

Give your answer to **3 significant figures**.

....

....

....

....

Answer = ... mm² **[4 marks]**

04.5 Some of the colonies are **not** perfectly circular.

Suggest what the student should do to work out the diameter of one of these colonies.

....

.... **[1 mark]**

05 Rose black spot is a fungal disease that affects plants.

It causes purple or black spots on leaves.

The leaves then often turn yellow and drop early.

05.1 Plants infected with rose black spot grow much more slowly than plants that are **not** infected.

Explain why the infected plants grow more slowly.

[3 marks]

05.2 Give **two** methods to prevent rose black spot from spreading, without destroying the plants.

Explain how each method works.

Method 1:

Explanation:

Method 2:

Explanation:

[4 marks]

Turn over >

06 Making monoclonal antibodies starts with combining mouse lymphocytes with tumour cells.

Figure 6.1 shows how this forms a hybridoma cell.

Figure 6.1

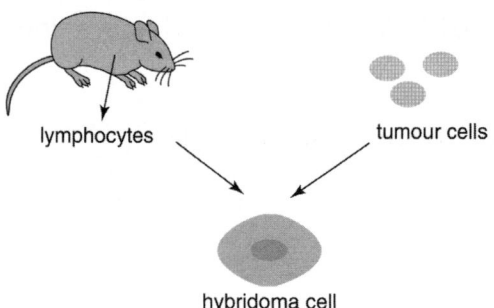

06.1 Explain why a hybridoma cell has to be made first in order to produce monoclonal antibodies.

[4 marks]

06.2 What do monoclonal antibodies bind to?

Tick **one** box.

Antibiotics ☐

Antibodies ☐

Antigens ☐

Antitoxins ☐

[1 mark]

06.3 Explain how monoclonal antibodies can be used to kill cancer cells.

....

....

....

[2 marks]

06.4 Explain the advantage of using monoclonal antibodies to kill cancer cells, compared with using other treatments.

....

....

[2 marks]

Turn over >

07 A student investigated osmosis using pieces of potato, and sucrose solutions of different concentrations.

This is the method used:

1. Cut pieces of potato of the same size and shape.
2. Measure the mass of each piece.
3. Leave each piece of potato in a different concentration of sucrose solution for one hour.
4. Remove each piece of potato, dry it with a cloth and measure its mass again.

Table 7.1 shows the student's results.

Table 7.1

Concentration of sucrose in mol per dm³	Mass of potato piece before being put in solution in g	Mass of potato piece after being put in solution in g	Percentage change in mass %
0.0	24.1	31.6	+31.1
0.2	24.0	29.0	
0.4	24.2	23.7	−2.1
0.6	23.9	19.3	−19.2
0.8	24.1	19.0	−21.2

07.1 Calculate the percentage change in mass for the potato in the 0.2 mol per dm³ sucrose solution.

Percentage change: .... % **[3 marks]**

07.2 Plot the data from **Table 7.1** and your answer to 07.1 onto **Figure 7.1**

Draw a smooth curved line of best fit.

Figure 7.1

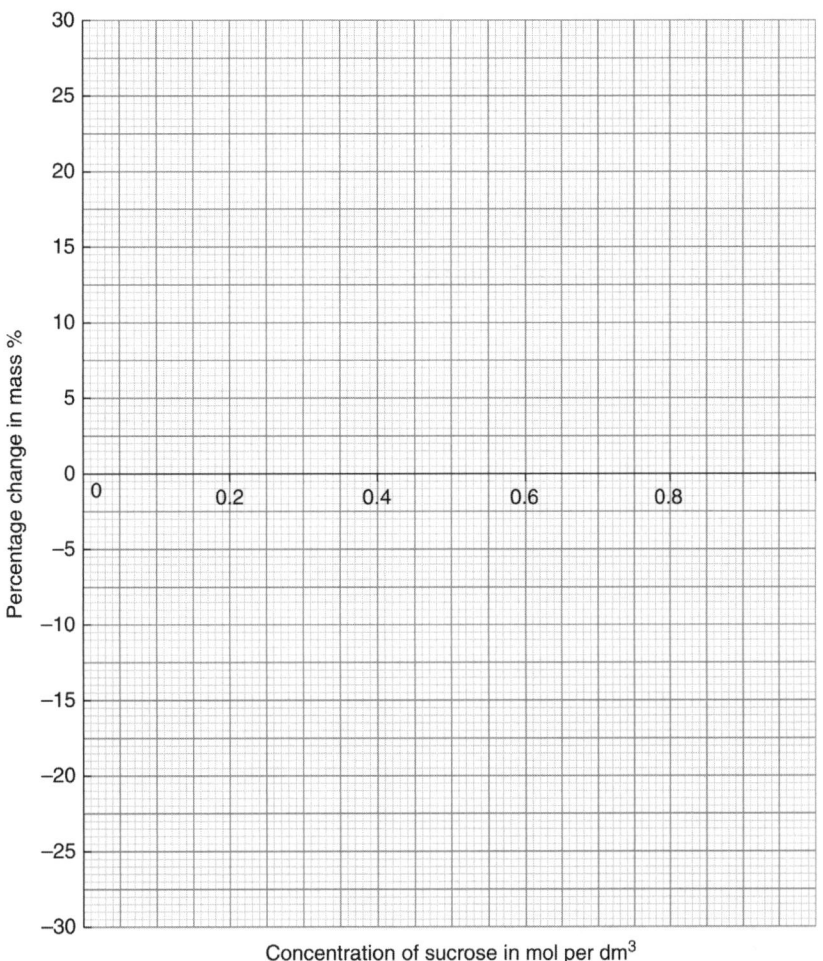

[3 marks]

07.3 Look at **Figure 7.1**

What concentration of sucrose would have the same concentration of water molecules as in the pieces of potato?

Answer: _____ mol per dm³   **[1 mark]**

Question 7 continues on the next page

07.4 Why was it important to cut all the pieces of potato to be as near as possible the same size and shape?

....

....

....
[2 marks]

07.5 Why was it important to dry each piece of potato before measuring its mass a second time?

....

....
[1 mark]

08 **Figure 8.1** shows some insects feeding on a rose plant in a garden.

The insects feed by putting their mouthparts into the plant's phloem tissue.

Figure 8.1

08.1 Suggest why the insects feed from the phloem tissue.

....

.... **[1 mark]**

08.2 Describe **two** ways in which the structure of phloem tissue is different from the structure of xylem tissue.

1. ....

....

2. ....

.... **[2 marks]**

Question 8 continues on the next page

08.3 A gardener might use a guidebook to identify the insects as aphids.

Suggest why identifying the insects might be useful for a gardener.

....

....
[1 mark]

08.4 During a hot day, rose plant leaves start to droop.

The stomata in the leaves close.

Explain why the stomata close.

Explain why this might also be a disadvantage for the plant.

....

....

....

....

....
[4 marks]

08.5 A gardener buys some insecticide liquid to kill aphids.

The instructions tell the gardener to pour the insecticide onto the soil around the plant.

The insecticide is taken in with water from the soil and travels to the top of the plant.

Describe how the insecticide will get from the soil to the top of the plant.

....

....

....

....
[3 marks]

09 Many diseases can be affected by lifestyle factors such as diet.

09.1 Explain why a diet that is too high in fat may lead to coronary heart disease.

[4 marks]

Question 9 continues on the next page

09.2 **Figure 9.1** shows data for obesity and Type 2 diabetes.

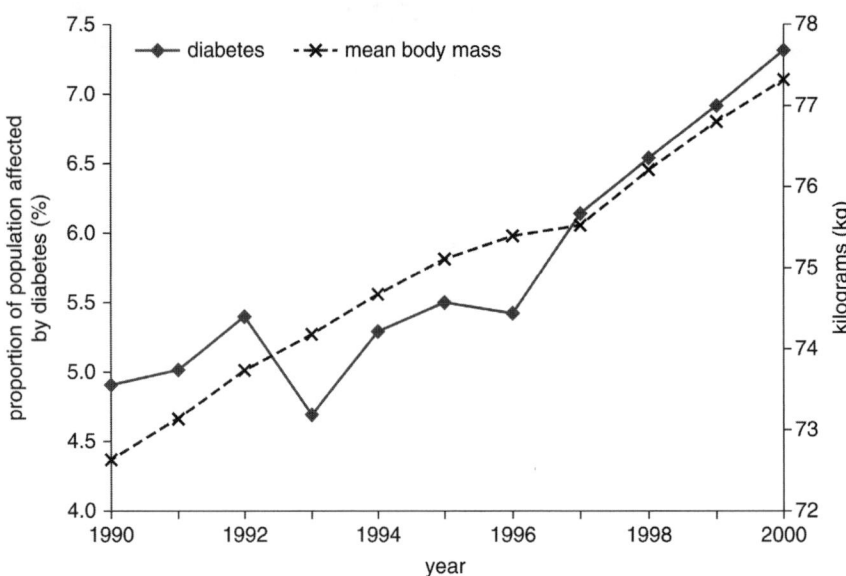

Figure 9.1

Evaluate whether the data from **Figure 9.1** shows that obesity is a risk factor for Type 2 diabetes.

[6 marks]

10 Figure 10.1 shows the effects of different limiting factors on the rate of photosynthesis.

Figure 10.1

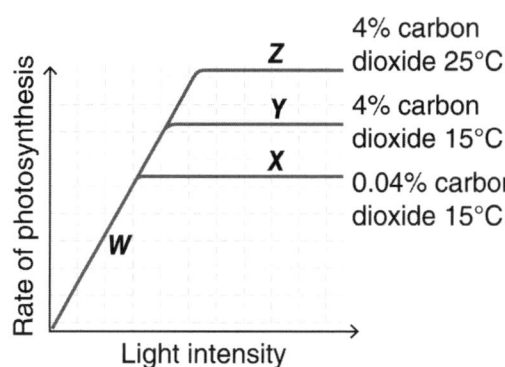

10.1 Identify the limiting factors at points **W**, **X** and **Y** on **Figure 10.1**

Explain the reasons for your answers.

Limiting factor at point **W**: ....

Explanation: ....

....

Limiting factor at point **X**: ....

Explanation: ....

....

Limiting factor at point **Y**: ....

Explanation: ....

.... **[6 marks]**

Question 10 continues on the next page

10.2 Without more information, it is **not** possible to identify the limiting factor at point **Z**.

Explain how you could identify the limiting factor at point **Z**.

[6 marks]

END OF QUESTIONS

Collins

AQA
GCSE
Biology
SET A – Paper 2 Higher Tier

H

Author: Mike Smith

Materials

Time allowed: 1 hour 45 minutes

For this paper you must have:
- a ruler
- a calculator.

Instructions

- Answer **all** questions in the spaces provided.
- Do all rough work in this book. Cross through any work you do not want to be marked.

Information

- There are 100 marks available on this paper.
- The marks for questions are shown in brackets.
- You are expected to use a calculator where appropriate.
- You are reminded of the need for good English and clear presentation in your answers.
- When answering questions 02.4, 03.1, 10.1 and 11.1 you need to make sure that your answer:
  – is clear, logical, sensibly structured
  – fully meets the requirements of the question
  – shows that each separate point or step supports the overall answer.

Advice

- In all calculations, show clearly how you work out your answer.

Name:

01 A student was investigating the effect of gravity on plant growth.

She grew some cress seeds on wet cotton wool in a Petri dish.

When the cress seedlings started to grow, the student turned the dish on its side.

Figure 1.1 shows the results.

Figure 1.1

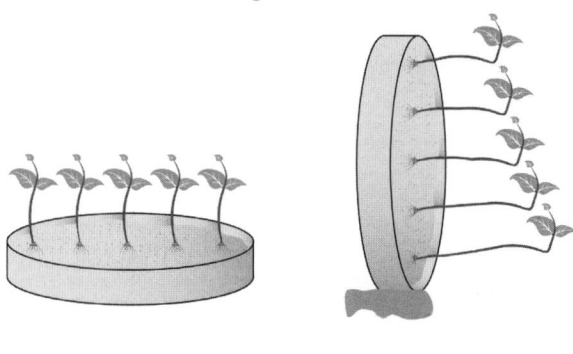

At start

One day after being turned on its side

01.1 State **one** variable the student should control.

Describe how it should be controlled.

Explain why it is important to control it.

Variable: ....

How variable should be controlled: ....

....

....

Why it is important to control the variable: ....

....

....

[3 marks]

01.2 Explain why it was important to grow more than one seedling.

....

....

[1 mark]

01.3 The seedlings grew upwards because of the effect of gravity.

This is controlled by a hormone called auxin.

Auxin moves downwards under the effect of gravity.

Explain how auxin caused the seedlings to grow upwards after the dish was turned on its side.

[2 marks]

01.4 The student repeated the experiment.

All the conditions were kept the same as the first time, **except** this time the dish was placed on a device which rotated the dish.

This is shown in **Figure 1.2**

Figure 1.2

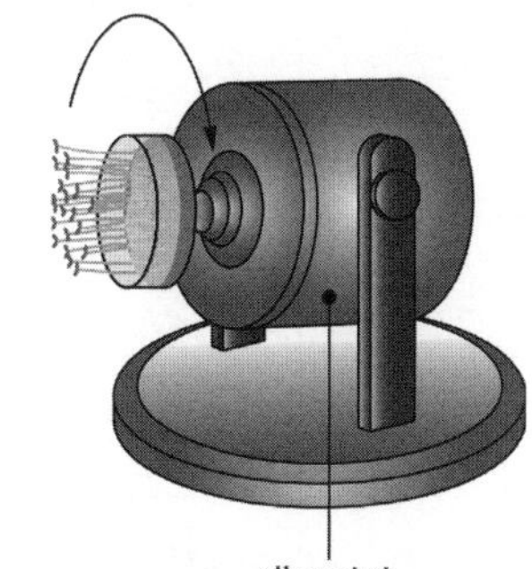

clinostat

Describe how you would expect the cress seedlings to grow this time.

Explain why the cress seedlings would grow this way.

[3 marks]

02 In a park, some grassland is left to grow wild except for a path which is mown regularly.

Students used a transect line to investigate how the path affected the distribution of four different plant species.

Figure 2.1 shows the line of the transect.

The students placed quadrats every metre along the transect.

Figure 2.1

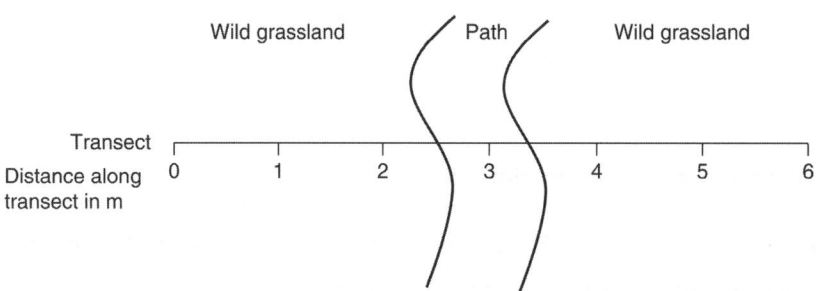

Table 2.1 shows their results.

Table 2.1

Distance along transect in m		0	1	2	3	4	5	6
Number of individual plants of each species per quadrat	Species A	10	8	6	0	8	12	10
	Species B	0	0	2	16	4	0	0
	Species C	8	6	4	0	6	8	8
	Species D	0	0	4	6	2	0	0

02.1 Look at **Table 2.1**

What is the mode number per quadrat for species D?

Answer: .... [1 mark]

02.2 Look at **Table 2.1**

What is the median number per quadrat for species A?

Answer: _____ [1 mark]

02.3 **Figure 2.2** shows kite diagrams of the results.

Use the data for **species A** from **Table 2.1** to complete **Figure 2.2**

Figure 2.2

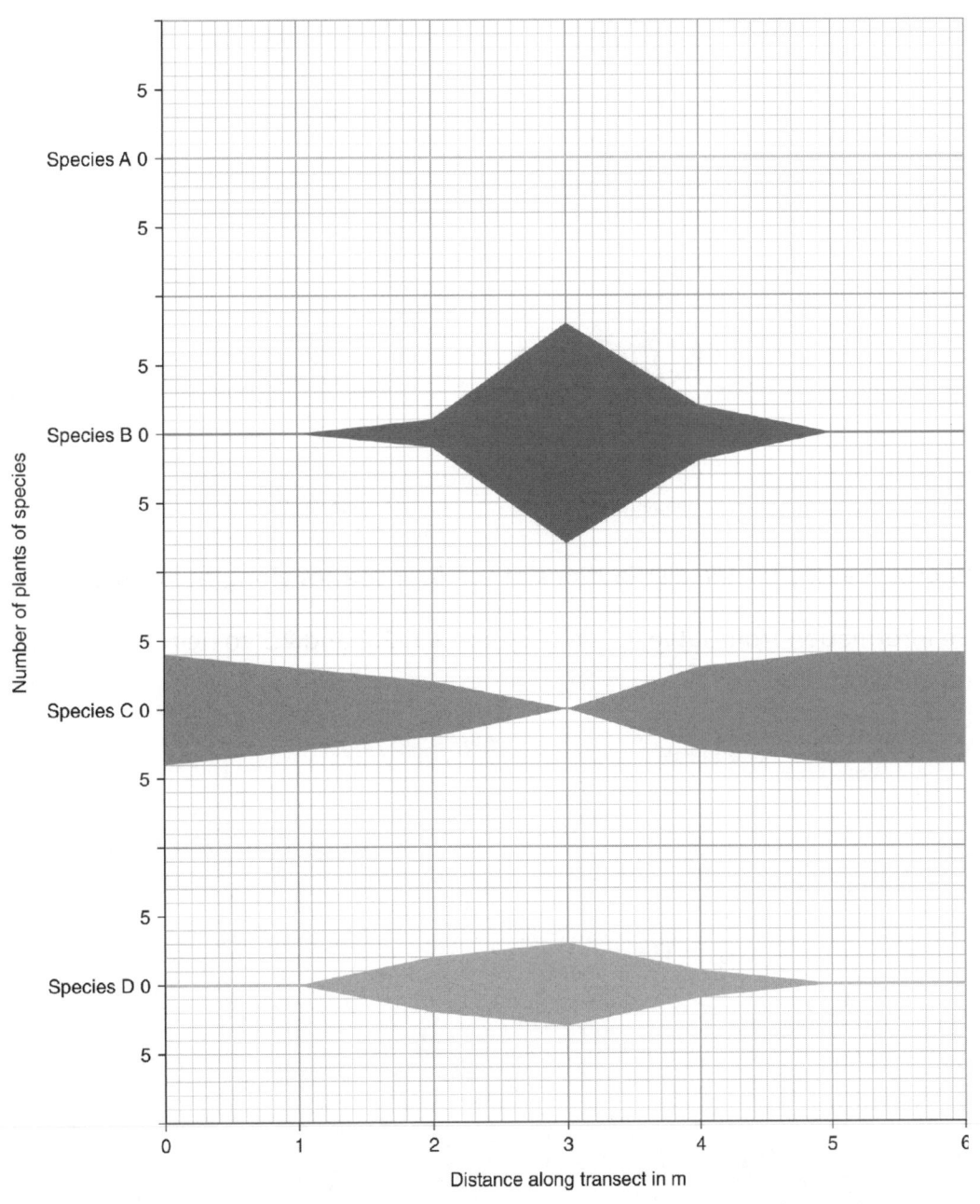

[4 marks]

Question 2 continues on the next page

02.4 **Figure 2.3** shows pictures of each plant species.

Figure 2.3

Species A

Species C

Species B

Species D

Suggest reasons for the distributions of the four species along the transect.

Use information from **Table 2.1** and **Figures 2.1**, **2.2** and **2.3** to help you answer.

[4 marks]

03 A group of students investigated their reaction times.

They each took it in turn to press a timer button as soon as they heard a buzzer.

Each student used their right hand.

Each student took the test three times and recorded their shortest reaction time.

There were eight girls and six boys in the group.

Table 3.1 shows their results.

Table 3.1

	Shortest reaction times in s								Mean reaction time in s
Girls	0.21	0.16	0.18	0.19	0.18	0.16	0.20	0.19	0.18
Boys	0.19	0.15	0.32	0.16	0.17	0.20			0.20

03.1 One of the students made this conclusion:

Girls have shorter reaction times than boys.

Evaluate the method used and the student's conclusion.

[6 marks]

Question 3 continues on the next page

03.2 **Figure 3.1** shows the nerve pathway involved in the investigation.

Figure 3.1

Sound of buzzer ⟶ Ear ⟶ Brain ⟶ Hand muscles ⟶ Press button

In **Figure 3.1**, which is the receptor and which is the effector?

Receptor: ....

Effector: .... **[2 marks]**

03.3 How does information pass along a nerve pathway?

....

.... **[2 marks]**

03.4 One of the students says:

Pressing the button quickly is an example of a reflex action.

Is the student correct?

Give a reason for your answer.

Is the student correct? ....

Reason: ....

.... **[1 mark]**

04 Cells can divide by mitosis or meiosis.

04.1 **Table 4.1** shows some features of mitosis or meiosis.

Complete **Table 4.1** by putting a tick (✓) or cross (✗) in each of the empty boxes.

Table 4.1

	Mitosis	Meiosis
Involved in body growth		
New cells produced have two copies of each chromosome		
Produces gametes		
Produces genetically identical cells		

[2 marks]

04.2 **Figure 4.1** shows some of the stages of a cell dividing by meiosis.

Write numbers **1**, **2**, **3** and **4** in the boxes to show the correct sequence.

Figure 4.1

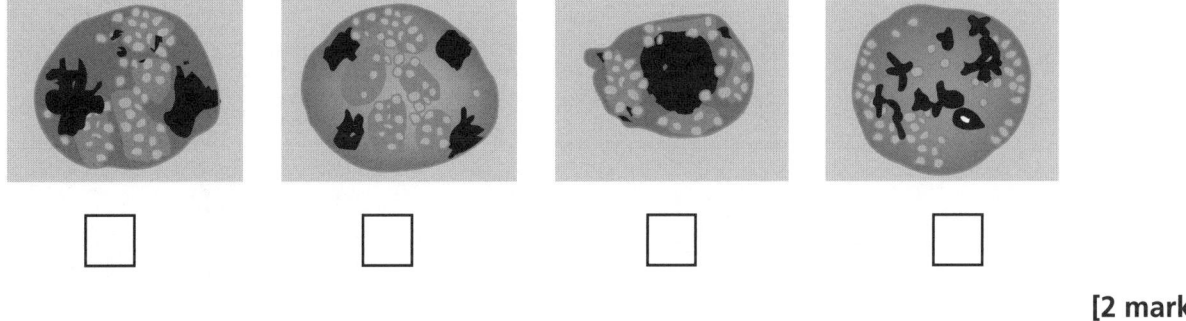

[2 marks]

Question 4 continues on the next page

04.3 Human males have the genotype **XY** and human females have the genotype **XX**.

What is the probability of a couple having a baby girl?

Draw a genetic diagram to explain your answer.

Probability = _____ [4 marks]

04.4 A couple already have one baby girl.

What is the probability that their next baby will also be a girl?

_____ [1 mark]

05 *In vitro* fertilisation (IVF) includes the following steps.

1. The hormones FSH (follicle stimulating hormone) and LH (luteinising hormone) are given to the mother.
2. Eggs are collected from the mother and sperm from the father.
3. The fertilised eggs develop into embryos.
4. Several embryos are inserted into the mother's uterus.

05.1 Explain why the mother is given FSH and LH.

[1 mark]

05.2 Where does fertilisation take place?

[1 mark]

05.3 Usually several embryos are inserted into the mother.

Explain why more than one embryo is inserted.

Describe the possible disadvantages of inserting several embryos.

Reason:

Disadvantages:

[4 marks]

Question 5 continues on the next page

05.4 **Figure 5.1** shows how the levels of four hormones vary during the menstrual cycle.

Figure 5.1

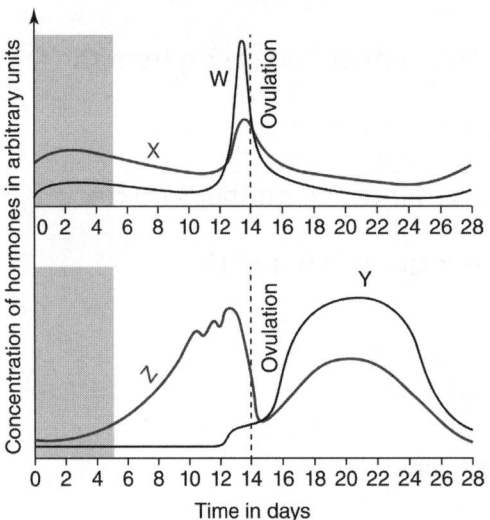

Write down the correct letter for each hormone.

FSH = _____

LH = _____

Oestrogen = _____

Progesterone = _____ **[3 marks]**

06 The amount of water in the body is controlled by a negative feedback system.

06.1 Figure 6.1 shows part of this negative feedback system.

Complete the missing words.

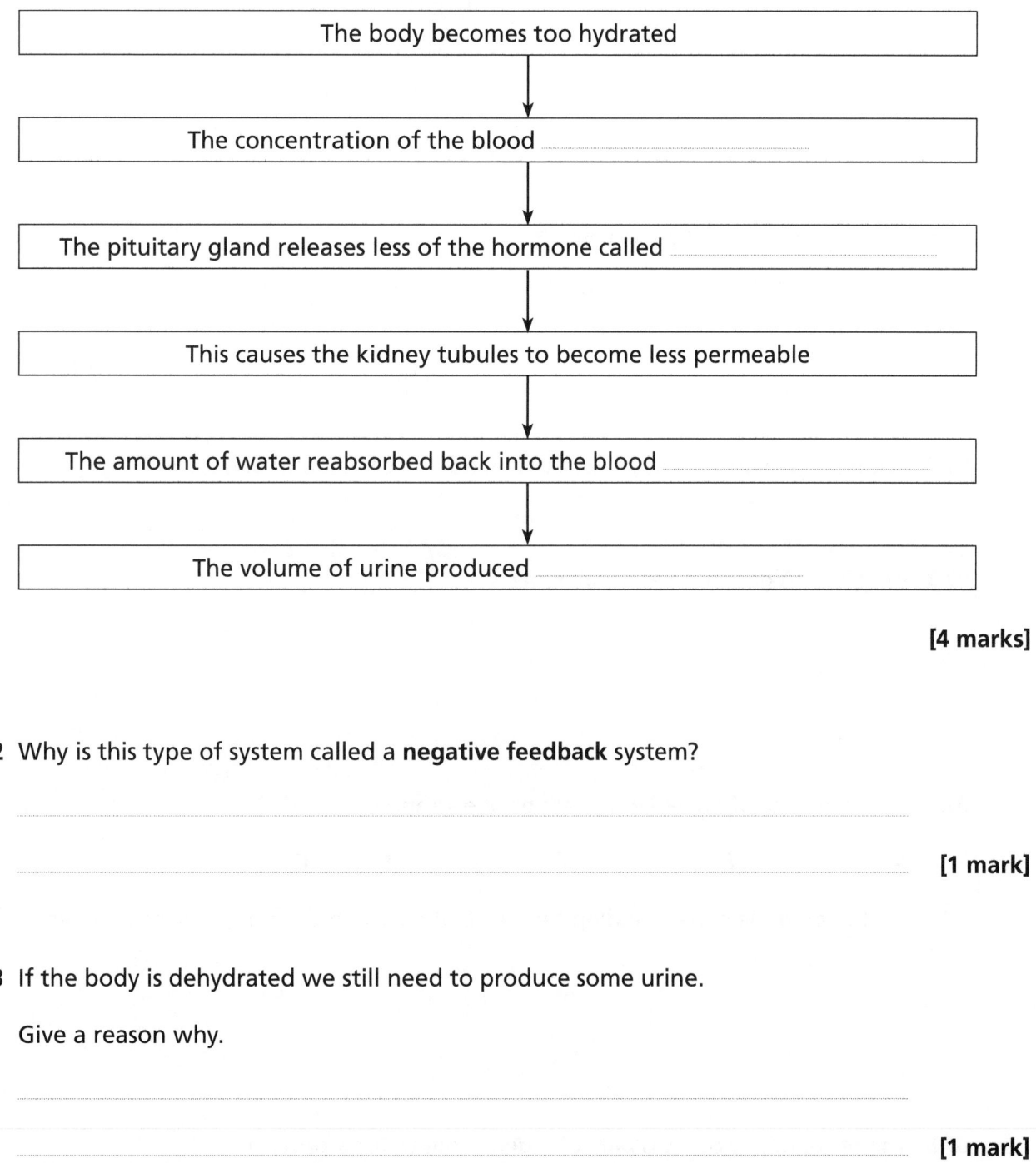

[4 marks]

06.2 Why is this type of system called a **negative feedback** system?

[1 mark]

06.3 If the body is dehydrated we still need to produce some urine.

Give a reason why.

[1 mark]

Turn over >

07   Figure 7.1 shows part of a DNA molecule.

Figure 7.1

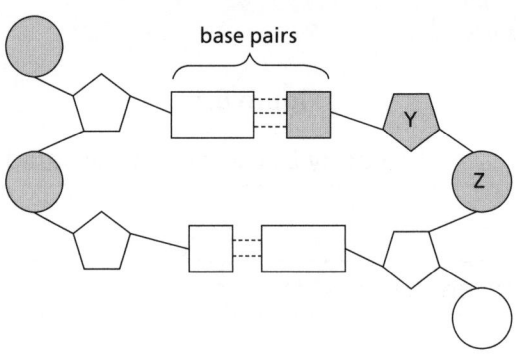

07.1   Identify the parts labelled **Y** and **Z**.

Y = _____

Z = _____   **[2 marks]**

07.2   What is the name of the shaded part made up of **Y**, **Z** and **one base**?

_____   **[1 mark]**

07.3   Why is DNA described as a **polymer**?   **[1 mark]**

_____

_____

07.4   The sequence of bases along part of one strand is:

A   T   T   C   G   C   T   C   A

Write down the corresponding sequence of bases on the complementary strand.

                                                                    [2 marks]

_____

07.5   The sequence of bases is part of a gene coding for a protein.

How many amino acids are coded for by the following sequence?

A   T   T   C   G   C   T   C   A   **[1 mark]**

_____

08 Polydactyly is a condition in which a person has extra fingers or toes.

It is an inherited disorder caused by a dominant allele **D**.

The recessive allele is **d**.

08.1 What is the genotype of someone who is heterozygous for polydactyly? **[1 mark]**

08.2 What is the genotype of someone who is homozygous for polydactyly?

[1 mark]

08.3 What is the phenotype of someone with the genotype **dd**? **[1 mark]**

08.4 Is it possible for two parents who do **not** have the polydactyly condition to have a child with the condition?

Explain your answer. **[2 marks]**

Answer:

Explanation:

Question 8 continues on the next page

08.5 **Figure 8.1** shows a family tree in which polydactyly occurs.

Figure 8.1

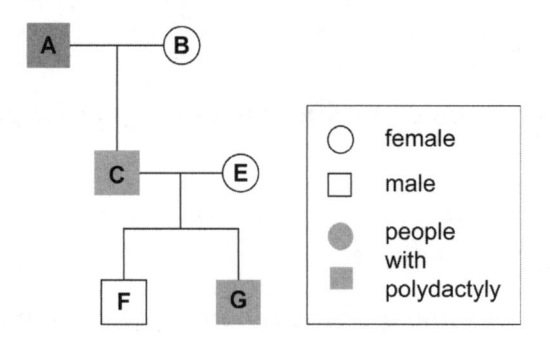

What are the possible genotypes of **A** and **C**?

Give reasons for your answers.

A = ...

C = ...

Reasons: ....

....

....

....

....

[4 marks]

08.6 Unlike polydactyly, most other inherited disorders are caused by **recessive** alleles.

Suggest why inherited disorders are more commonly caused by recessive alleles.

....

....

[1 mark]

09 Figure 9.1 shows a type of bird called a St Kilda wren.

Figure 9.1

St Kilda wrens live on the island of St Kilda off the north coast of Scotland.

They are similar to wrens that live on the mainland, but St Kilda wrens are larger.

Wrens are too small to normally fly to or from the island.

Scientists think that:

- St Kilda wrens are descended from mainland wrens that were blown over to the island by strong winds
- their larger size is an adaptation to help keep warm.

09.1 Scientists think that the St Kilda wrens have evolved from mainland wrens by natural selection.

Describe how this may have happened.

[4 marks]

Question 9 continues on the next page

09.2 Although St Kilda wrens are different from the mainland wrens they are classified as the **same** species.

Describe how you could show that the mainland wrens and the St Kilda wrens are the same species.

....

....

.... **[2 marks]**

09.3 The mainland wrens have the scientific name *Troglodytes troglodytes*.

The St Kilda wrens have the scientific name *Troglodytes troglodytes hirtensis*.

Suggest why the St Kilda wrens have this different scientific name.

....

....

.... **[2 marks]**

09.4 In the future, the St Kilda wrens may evolve to become so different from the mainland wrens that they could be classified as a different species.

Which of the following could be an appropriate name for the new species?

Tick **one** box and give a reason for your answer.

Hirtensis hirtensis ☐

Hirtensis troglodytes ☐

Troglodytes hirtensis ☐

Troglodytes troglodytes ☐

Reason: ....

....

.... **[2 marks]**

10 **Figure 10.1** shows two ways that humans get their food.

The size of the arrows represents how much energy or biomass is transferred to each trophic level.

Figure 10.1

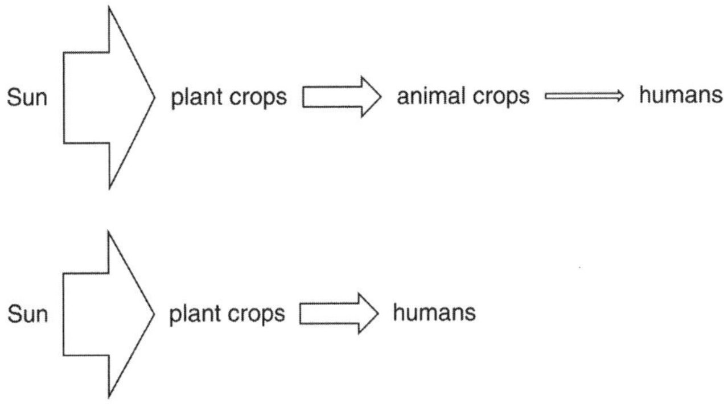

Sun ⟹ plant crops ⟹ animal crops ⟹ humans

Sun ⟹ plant crops ⟹ humans

10.1 Use information from **Figure 10.1** and your own knowledge to help you:

- compare the efficiency of humans feeding at different trophic levels, giving reasons for the differences

- suggest any implications this may have for the diets of humans as the human population continues to increase.

[6 marks]

Question 10 continues on the next page

10.2 The body of a fish:

- is the same temperature as the water it swims in
- is supported by water, so it does **not** need to use as much energy to move as an animal on land.

Use this information, **Figure 10.1** and your own knowledge to help you explain this statement:

Food chains involving fish are usually longer than food chains involving animals living on land.

[2 marks]

11 Bylot Island is in the Arctic.

Not many animal species live on Bylot Island.

Two species that do live there are snowy owls and lemmings as shown in **Figure 11.1**

Snowy owls catch and eat lemmings.

Figure 11.1

Snowy owl   Lemming

11.1 **Figure 11.2** shows data from Bylot Island.

Figure 11.2

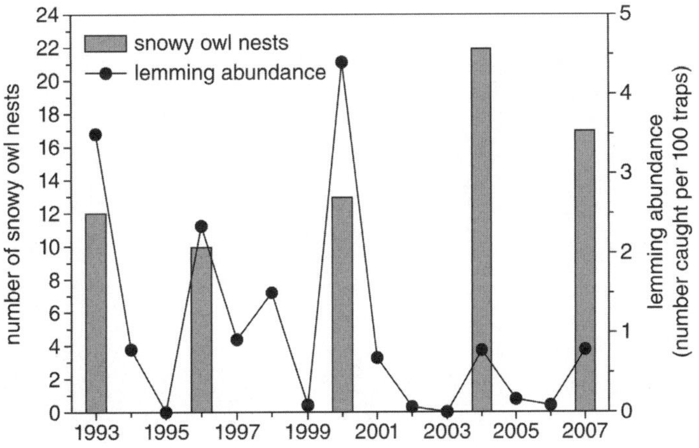

Question 11 continues on the next page

Describe any patterns in the data shown in **Figure 11.2**

Suggest explanations for these patterns.

[6 marks]

11.2 Snowy owl bodies contain carbon.

Eventually this carbon is recycled back into the atmosphere as carbon dioxide.

Describe how this happens.

[3 marks]

11.3 Bylot Island has a low biodiversity.

Student **A** says:

It is important to protect places like Bylot Island.

Student **B** says:

It is more important to protect places with a higher biodiversity like tropical rainforest.

Explain why these two statements are both valid.

[2 marks]

END OF QUESTIONS

BLANK PAGE

Collins

AQA
GCSE
Biology
SET B – Paper 1 Higher Tier

H

Author: Kath Skillern

Materials

For this paper you must have:
- a ruler
- a calculator.

Time allowed: 1 hour 45 minutes

Instructions

- Answer **all** questions in the spaces provided.
- Do all rough work in this book. Cross through any work you do not want to be marked.

Information

- There are 100 marks available on this paper.
- The marks for questions are shown in brackets.
- You are expected to use a calculator where appropriate.
- You are reminded of the need for good English and clear presentation in your answers.
- When answering questions 07.3 and 09.3 you need to make sure that your answer:
  – is clear, logical, sensibly structured
  – fully meets the requirements of the question
  – shows that each separate point or step supports the overall answer.

Advice

- In all calculations, show clearly how you work out your answer.

Name: _____

01 Herbivores, pests and pathogens often destroy leaves and other parts of the plant.

Plant defences minimise this damage.

01.1 Which of the following is a **chemical** plant defence response?

Tick **one** box.

Bark ☐

Cellulose cell walls ☐

Poison ☐

Waxy cuticle ☐

[1 mark]

01.2 Describe the action of **two mechanical** plant defence responses.

Explain how each of them works.

_____

_____

_____

_____

[4 marks]

01.3 Name **two** non-specific physical or chemical barriers that defend the body from infection.

_____

[2 marks]

01.4 Describe **two** ways white blood cells help defend the human body against pathogens.

_____

_____

[2 marks]

02 Pathogens cause diseases in plants and animals.

Plants and animals are able to defend themselves against attack.

02.1 Name a plant disease that is caused by a virus.

....
[1 mark]

02.2 Explain how this virus affects the whole plant.

....

....

....
[3 marks]

02.3 Name a plant disease that is caused by a fungus.

....
[1 mark]

02.4 Plants can also be damaged by ion deficiency.

Name an ion deficiency condition in plants.

Describe **one** effect of this deficiency.

Explain why this effect occurs.

....

....

....
[3 marks]

03 The digestive system is a collection of organs that work together to digest and absorb food.

03.1 What is the name given to biological molecules that break down our food?

Tick **one** box.

Catalysts ☐

Enzymes ☐

Proteins ☐

Substrate ☐

[1 mark]

03.2 Tom ate a sausage sandwich.

Complete the following sentences:

- Proteases break down _____ to _____ .
- Lipases break down _____ to glycerol and _____ .

[4 marks]

03.3 Amylase is a carbohydrase that breaks down starch to maltose and glucose.

Tom investigated the effect of pH on the rate of reaction of amylase.

This is the method used.

1. Gather three solutions:
   - amylase
   - starch solution
   - pH buffer solution.
2. Set up a spotting tile with rows of iodine drops and prepare the stopwatch.
3. Mix the three solutions in a test tube in a particular order and start the stopwatch.

Which is the correct order to put the solutions into the test tube?

.... [1 mark]

03.4 Explain why it is important that Tom mixed the solutions in the correct order.

....
....
.... [2 marks]

03.5 At 10 second intervals, Tom used a pipette to place a drop of the 3 solutions mix onto the next iodine drop in the spotting tile.

He repeated this until the iodine remained orange after the mix was added.

Describe how Tom could set up a colour control.

....
.... [1 mark]

03.6 Why might a control have helped Tom?

....
....
.... [2 marks]

Turn over >

04   **Figure 4.1** shows a virus and some different cells.

The diagrams are **not** to scale.

Figure 4.1

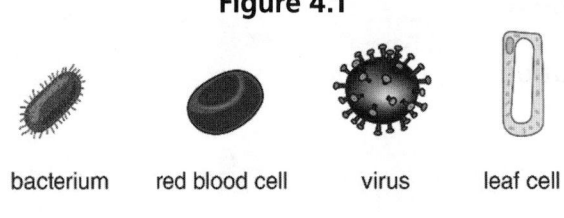

bacterium   red blood cell   virus   leaf cell

04.1 Write the items in order of their size, from the smallest to the largest.

Smallest ....

....

....

Largest ....   **[1 mark]**

04.2 Give **two** reasons for using a coverslip when looking at a slide under the microscope.

....

....   **[2 marks]**

04.3 When using a microscope, describe the difference between the field of view of a low-power lens with the field of view of a high-power lens.

Explain what causes this difference.

....

....   **[2 marks]**

04.4 Which stain is used to add colour and contrast to plant cells for viewing under the microscope?

Tick **one** box.

Hydrogen peroxide ☐

Iodine solution ☐

Methylene blue ☐

Potassium dichromate ☐   **[1 mark]**

04.5 A micrograph is a photograph taken using a microscope.

Figure 4.2 shows a low-power micrograph of a plant root. The root is approximately 2 mm in diameter just below the meristem.

Figure 4.2

Draw a diagram of the plant root.

Label the meristem on your diagram.

Draw an appropriate scale bar on your diagram.

[4 marks]

04.6 Explain why a plant meristem is described as a zone made up of stem cells.

[1 mark]

Turn over >

05 **Figure 5.1** shows the number of preventable cancers, linked to lifestyle choices, in the UK in 2011.

Figure 5.1

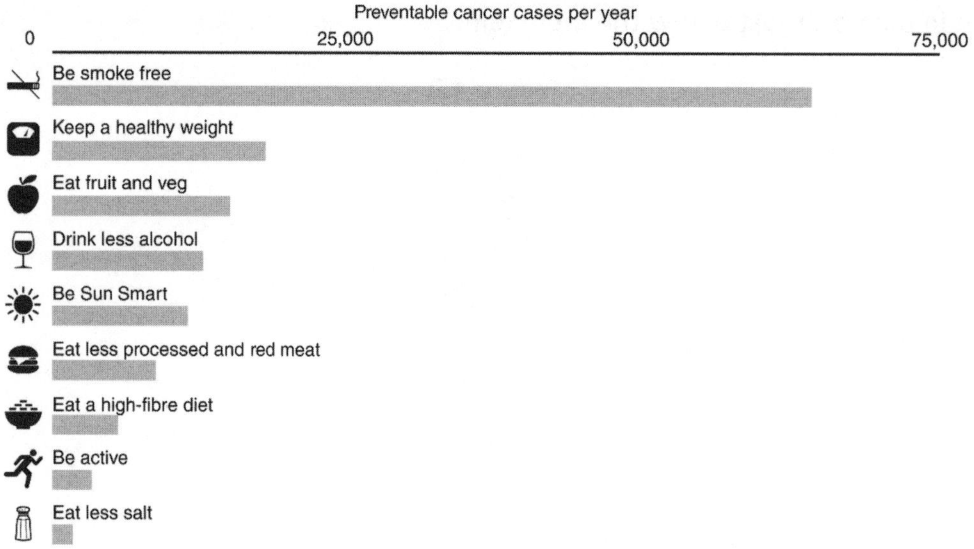
Preventable cancer cases per year
0
25,000
50,000
75,000
Be smoke free
Keep a healthy weight
Eat fruit and veg
Drink less alcohol
Be Sun Smart
Eat less processed and red meat
Eat a high-fibre diet
Be active
Eat less salt

05.1 How many preventable cancers were related to smoking?

.... **[1 mark]**

05.2 Compare the numbers of preventable cancers related to **being active** with those related to **drinking less alcohol.**

....

....

.... **[2 marks]**

05.3 Use the data in **Figure 5.1** to describe a healthy diet to reduce the risk of developing cancer.

....

.... **[2 marks]**

05.4 The most common types of cancers are different for men compared with women.

Suggest reasons for this.

....

....

....

.... **[3 marks]**

06 A vaccination introduces a small quantity of dead pathogen into the body to protect us from disease.

A new vaccination has been developed against the pathogen Lumpius.

The Lumpius vaccine is being tested by a pharmaceutical company, which has recruited 10 000 volunteers.

Figure 6.1 shows the body's response to the vaccination and later to infection by Lumpius.

Figure 6.1

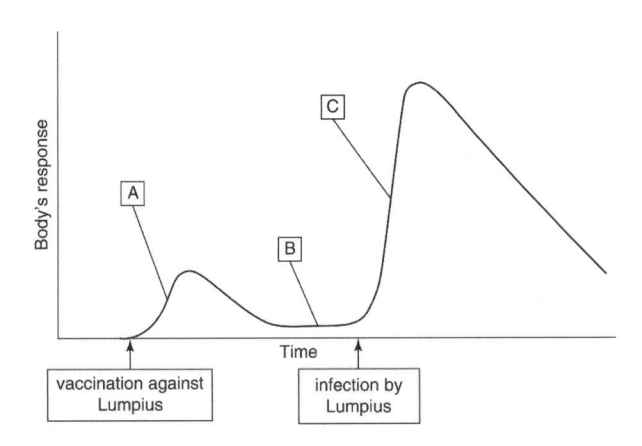

06.1 Describe what is happening at A.

[2 marks]

Question 6 continues on the next page

06.2 Describe what is happening at B.

....

.... **[1 mark]**

06.3 Describe what is happening at C.

....

....

.... **[3 marks]**

06.4 Use **Figure 6.1** to draw conclusions about:

- how effective the vaccine is
- the dose of the vaccine.

....

....

.... **[4 marks]**

06.5 At what stage of development is the vaccine?

Give a reason for your answer.

....

....

.... **[2 marks]**

07 Jane has set up equipment to investigate the rate of photosynthesis in an aquatic plant.

She uses a lamp as a light source.

Figure 7.1

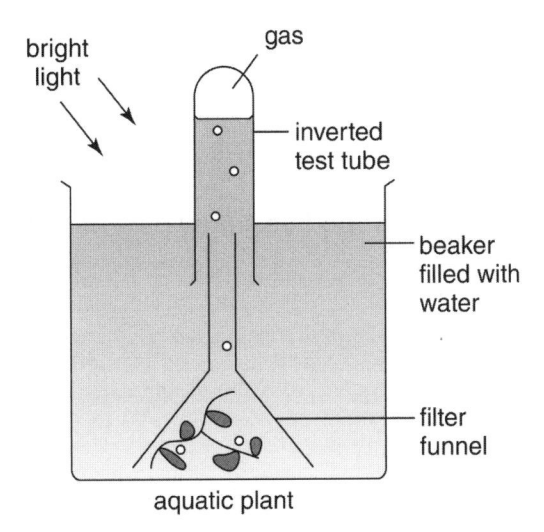

07.1 What is the name of the gas collecting in the test tube?

_____
[1 mark]

07.2 Jane uses a lamp as a light source.

Name **two** other pieces of equipment she will need.

_____

_____
[2 marks]

07.3 Explain how Jane should carry out her investigation.

_____

_____

_____

_____

_____

_____

_____
[6 marks]

Question 7 continues on the next page

07.4 What **additional** equipment could Jane use to measure the amount of gas more accurately?

....

....
[1 mark]

07.5 Jane wants a pond in her garden to keep fish.

Explain why she should dig her pond in a sunny part of the garden.

....

....
[2 marks]

07.6 **Figure 7.2** shows Jane's results.

Figure 7.2

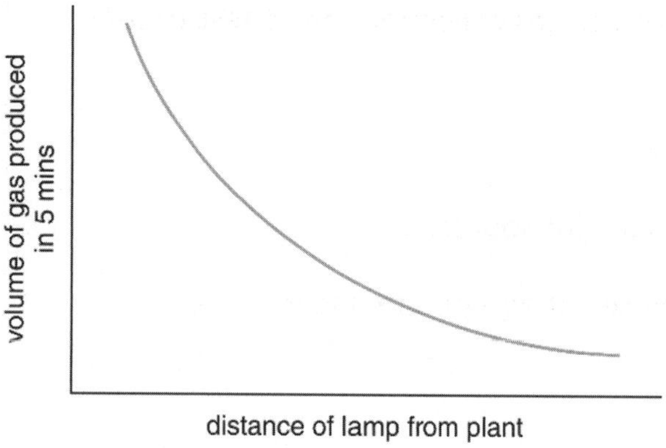

[Graph showing volume of gas produced in 5 mins (y-axis) against distance of lamp from plant (x-axis); curve decreases steeply then levels off]

Explain the shape of the graph.

....

....

....
[3 marks]

08 During long periods of vigorous activity, insufficient oxygen is supplied to the muscles and anaerobic respiration takes place.

An oxygen debt is created by a build-up of lactic acid.

08.1 Why does lactic acid build up in the muscles?

....
[1 mark]

08.2 Figure 8.1 shows oxygen consumption over time.

Figure 8.1

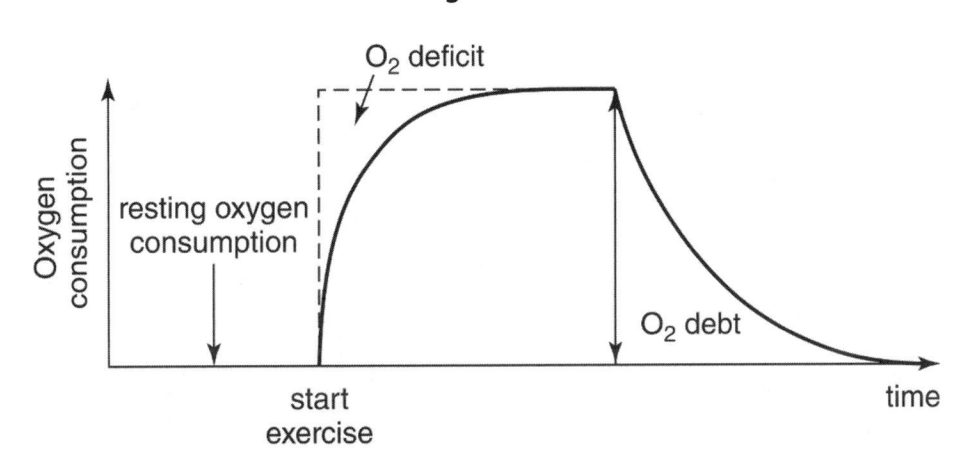

Add the following labels to the graph:

A. Excess post-exercise oxygen consumption

B. Steady state oxygen consumption

C. Oxygen requirement

D. Finish exercise

E. Recovery

[5 marks]

08.3 Describe what happens after exercising to the lactic acid that has built up in the muscles.

....

....
[2 marks]

Question 8 continues on the next page

08.4 Describe what is meant by 'oxygen debt', in terms of the amount of oxygen required by the body.

....

....

....
[2 marks]

08.5 **Figure 8.2** shows the effects of exercise on the heart rates of two people.

Figure 8.2

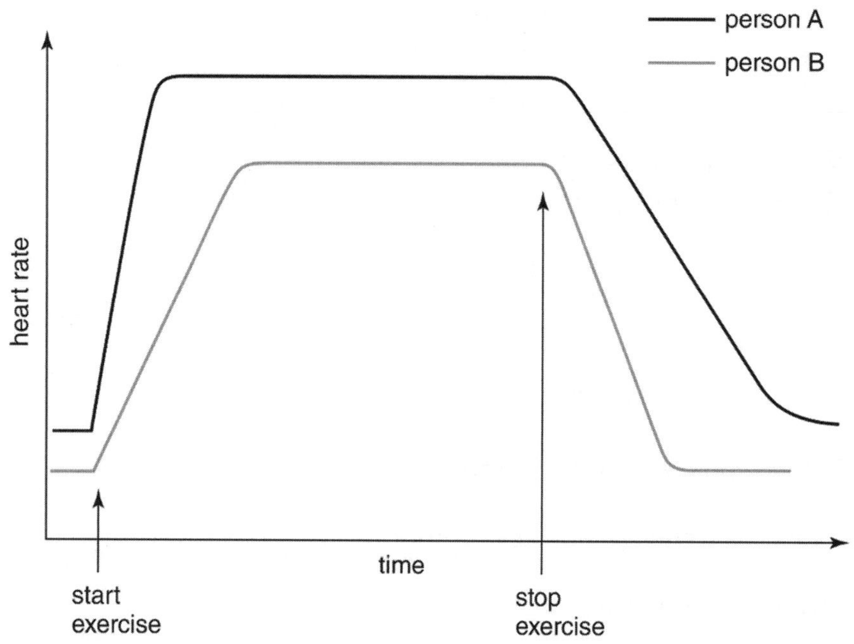

Which person is fitter?

Tick **one** box.

Person A ☐

Person B ☐
[1 mark]

08.6 Give **two** reasons for your answer.

....

....

....

....
[2 marks]

09 Metabolism is the sum of all the reactions in a cell or organism.

The energy transferred supplies all the energy needed for living processes.

One of these processes is respiration.

09.1 Energy from respiration is used in active transport.

What is active transport?

[2 marks]

09.2 What is another major use of the energy released from respiration?

[1 mark]

09.3 Describe other processes of metabolism.

[6 marks]

Turn over >

10 Stomata are small pores on the surface of plant leaves.

Plants open and close their stomata under different conditions.

10.1 Explain **one** advantage to a plant of closing its stomata.

....

.... **[2 marks]**

10.2 Explain **one** disadvantage to a plant of closing its stomata.

....

.... **[2 marks]**

… Collins

AQA
GCSE
Biology
SET B – Paper 2 Higher Tier

H

Author: Kath Skillern

Materials

Time allowed: 1 hour 45 minutes

For this paper you must have:
- a ruler
- a calculator.

Instructions
- Answer **all** questions in the spaces provided.
- Do all rough work in this book. Cross through any work you do not want to be marked.

Information
- There are 100 marks available on this paper.
- The marks for questions are shown in brackets.
- You are expected to use a calculator where appropriate.
- You are reminded of the need for good English and clear presentation in your answers.
- When answering questions 03.3, 04.6 and 06.3 you need to make sure that your answer:
  – is clear, logical, sensibly structured
  – fully meets the requirements of the question
  – shows that each separate point or step supports the overall answer.

Advice
- In all calculations, show clearly how you work out your answer.

Name:

01 An ecosystem is the interaction of a community of living organisms with the non-living parts of their environment.

01.1 How is the **non-living** part of the environment described?

Tick **one** box.

Abiotic ☐

Biotic ☐

Dead ☐

Habitat ☐

[1 mark]

01.2 Name **two** resources that **plants** compete for.

1. ....

2. .... [2 marks]

01.3 Name **two** resources that **animals** compete for.

1. ....

2. .... [2 marks]

01.4 Within a community each species depends on other species to help it survive.

If one species is removed it can affect the whole community.

How is this described?

.... [1 mark]

01.5 Explain the term 'a stable community'.

....

....

.... [2 marks]

01.6 Biological material eventually dies and decays.

What does **anaerobic** decay produce?

Tick **one** box.

Carbon dioxide ☐

Ethane ☐

Lactic acid ☐

Methane ☐ [1 mark]

01.7 Microorganisms return carbon dioxide to the atmosphere.

Which material do they return to the soil?

.... [1 mark]

02 The human body reacts to changes by coordinating a **nervous** response or a **hormonal** response.

02.1 Compare the body's nervous response with a hormonal response.

[4 marks]

02.2 In **Scientific Study A**, reaction times were investigated after four volunteers had drunk alcohol.

A small can of beer contains about one unit of alcohol.

The results are shown in **Table 2.1**

Table 2.1

Volunteer	Reaction time in milliseconds (ms)					
	Units of alcohol	0.5	1.5	3.0	4.5	6.0
A		34	45	59	71	85
B		35	47	62	75	87
C		32	46	64	72	83
D		30	42	59	70	
Mean		33	45	61	72	84

Calculate the reaction time of volunteer D after 6.0 units of alcohol

Reaction time of volunteer D after 6.0 units of alcohol = _____ [3 marks]

02.3 Use the results to describe how alcohol affects reaction time.

....

....

.... **[2 marks]**

02.4 In **Scientific Study B**, a test was carried out on 2000 people of all ages.

Comment on the repeatability of **Scientific Studies A and B**.

....

.... **[2 marks]**

03 Type 2 diabetes is a serious condition.

In Type 2 diabetes the body's cells no longer respond as effectively to control glucose concentration in the blood.

Look at **Table 3.1**

Table 3.1

Year	Percentage (%) of the population who have Type 2 diabetes	Mean body mass in kg
1990	4.9	72.5
1991	5.0	73.0
1992	5.4	73.7
1993	4.7	74.0
1994	5.3	74.6
1995	5.5	75.0
1996	5.4	74.8
1997	6.2	75.3
1998	6.5	76.0
1999	6.9	76.6
2000	7.3	77.2

03.1 Use the data in **Table 3.1** to plot a graph to show the effect of body mass on percentage of the population who have Type 2 diabetes.

You do not need to use the Year column in **Table 3.1**.

Make sure to:
- choose an appropriate scale
- label both axes
- plot all points to show the pattern of results.

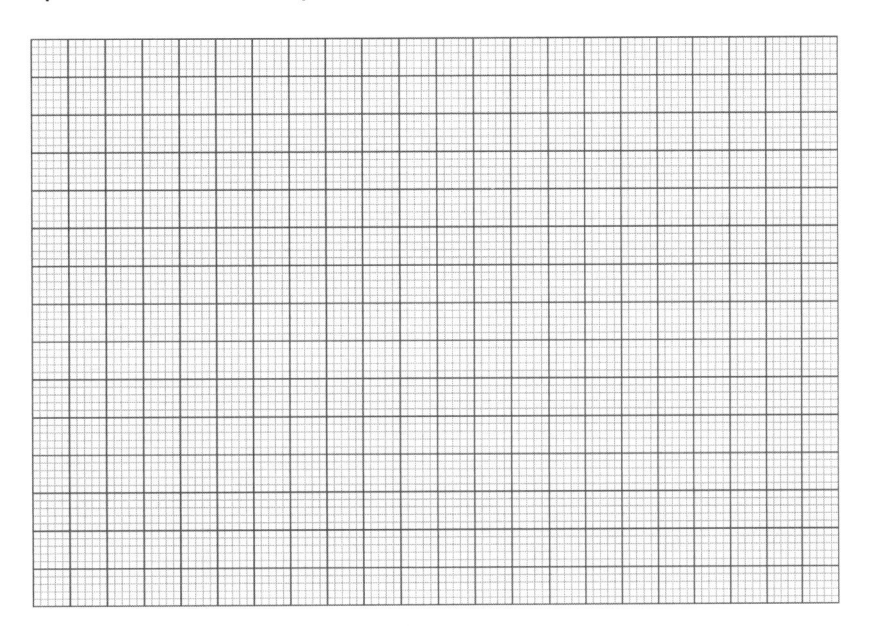

[4 marks]

03.2 Describe the relationship between the mean body mass of the population and the percentage of people who have **Type 2 diabetes**.

[1 mark]

Question 3 continues on the next page

03.3 If one person has Type 2 diabetes, and another person does not:

- explain how the negative feedback system in their bodies controls high levels of blood glucose concentration
- describe the differences in the blood glucose concentration of the two people after they have both eaten a full breakfast.

[6 marks]

04 Evolutionary trees are used by scientists to show how organisms are related.

Figure 4.1 shows an evolutionary tree.

The numbers on the branches of the evolutionary tree are the number of 'million years ago'.

Figure 4.1

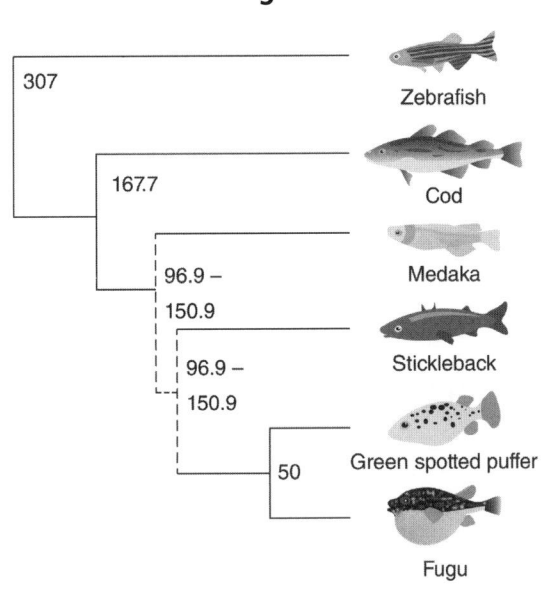

04.1 Which fish is the most **distantly** related to the others?

Tick **one** box

Cod ☐

Fugu ☐

Green spotted puffer ☐

Medaka ☐

Stickleback ☐

Zebrafish ☐

[1 mark]

Question 4 continues on the next page

04.2 Which **two** fishes are most **closely** related?

Tick **two** boxes

Cod ☐

Fugu ☐

Green spotted puffer ☐

Medaka ☐

Stickleback ☐

Zebrafish ☐

[1 mark]

04.3 How long ago did the cod split from medaka and stickleback?

.... [1 mark]

04.4 Suggest why there is only a **dotted** line between medaka and stickleback.

....

.... [1 mark]

04.5 Name **one** type of evidence that helps scientists construct evolutionary trees.

.... [1 mark]

04.6 Describe the steps which may have given rise to medaka and stickleback becoming different species.

[6 marks]

05 **Figure 5.1** shows a section through a human brain.

Figure 5.1

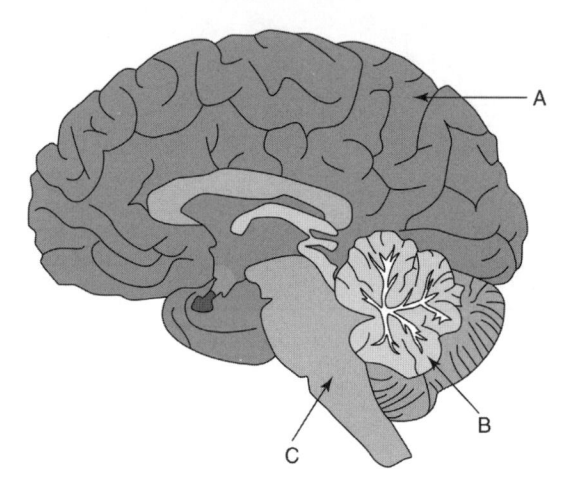

05.1 What is the area labelled **A** on **Figure 5.1**?

Tick **one** box

Cerebellum ☐

Cerebral cortex ☐

Medusa ☐

Pituitary ☐

[1 mark]

05.2 What is the area labelled **B** on **Figure 5.1**?

Tick **one** box

Cerebellum ☐

Cerebral cortex ☐

Hypothalamus ☐

Medulla ☐

[1 mark]

05.3 What is the area labelled **C** on **Figure 5.1**?

Tick **one** box

Medulla ☐

Medusa ☐

Optic nerve ☐

Spinal column ☐ [1 mark]

05.4 What is the function of area **A**, area **B** and area **C**?

Give **one** example for each.

Area A

Function: _____

Example: _____

Area B

Function: _____

Example: _____

Area C

Function: _____

Example: _____ [6 marks]

Question 5 continues on the next page

05.5 **Figure 5.2** shows the brain weight and body mass of animals.

Figure 5.2

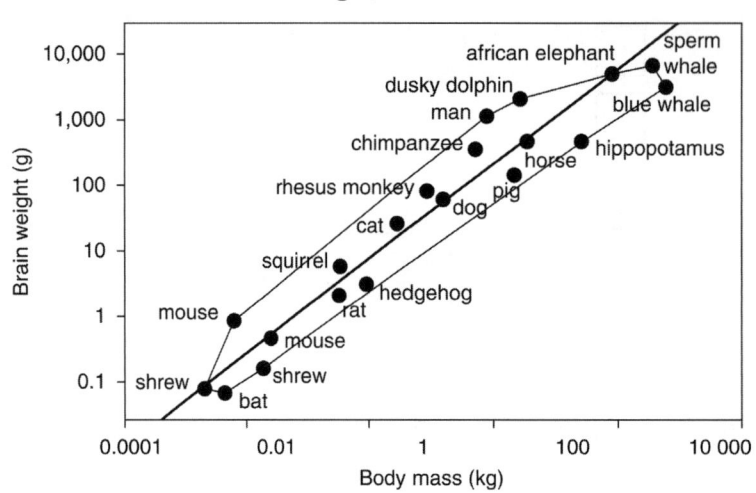

[Scatter graph: Brain weight (g) on y-axis (0.1 to 10,000, logarithmic) vs Body mass (kg) on x-axis (0.0001 to 10 000, logarithmic). Animals plotted include: shrew, bat, mouse, shrew, mouse, rat, hedgehog, squirrel, cat, rhesus monkey, dog, pig, chimpanzee, horse, man, dusky dolphin, hippopotamus, african elephant, blue whale, sperm whale.]

Describe the relationship between the size of an animal and the size of its brain.

....

....

....

....
[2 marks]

05.6 Suggest **one** reason for this relationship.

....

....
[1 mark]

05.7 Suggest **one** reason why this relationship is not seen **within a species**.

....

....
[1 mark]

06 DNA contains four bases.

06.1 Which base does A (adenine) always pair with?

....
[1 mark]

06.2 How many bases code for a single amino acid?

....
[1 mark]

06.3 A disease called Leigh syndrome occurs when the process of protein synthesis is disrupted, causing the wrong protein to be made.

Explain how the process of protein synthesis might be disrupted in Leigh syndrome.

....
....
....
....
....
....
....
....
....
....
....
....
[6 marks]

Question 6 continues on the next page

06.4 Give **two** applications for our understanding of the human genome.

[2 marks]

07 **Figure 7.1** shows five closely related species of fish, with their diets and habitats.

Figure 7.1

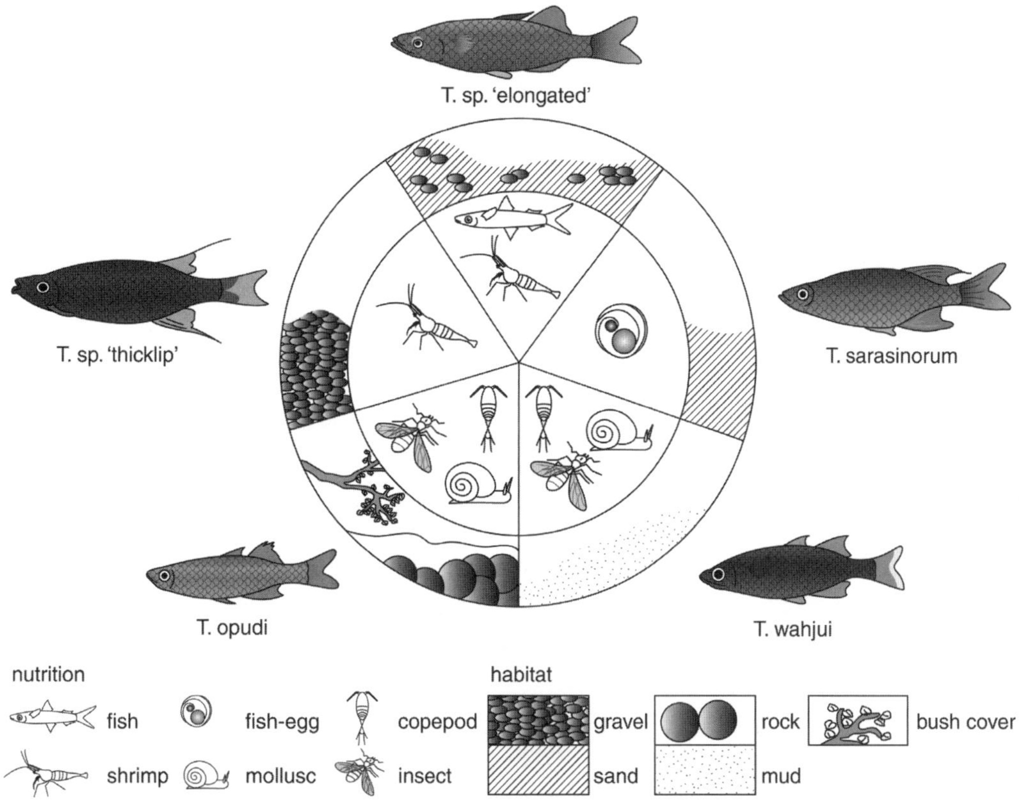

07.1 The copepods in this community are primary consumers.

Suggest what their diet may consist of.

_____ **[1 mark]**

Question 7 continues on the next page

07.2 In one year, there was a huge increase in numbers of *T. sarasinorum*.

How would this affect the numbers of 'thicklip'?

Explain your answer.

[3 marks]

07.3 Explain why *T. opudi* and *T. wahjui* are **not** competitors, even though they have similar diets.

[2 marks]

07.4 Name a source of pollution that could affect the fish.

[1 mark]

07.5 Explain why pyramids of biomass are rarely higher than four organisms.

[3 marks]

08 In the year 2000, a litter of piglets was produced by cloning.

One of the piglets born was called Millie.

Figure 8.1 shows the cloning of Millie the piglet.

Figure 8.1

Question 8 continues on the next page

08.1 Look at **Figure 8.1**

Suggest labels to describe the cloning process at points **A, B, C, D** and **E**.

A ....

B ....

C ....

D ....

E .... **[5 marks]**

08.2 In the year 2001, a kitten called Copy Cat was produced by cloning.

Copy Cat was genetically identical to the cloned cat, but the patterns on her fur were different.

Suggest a reason for this.

....

.... **[1 mark]**

08.3 Name **two** different types of organism that naturally produce clones.

....

.... **[2 marks]**

08.4 Give **two** advantages of this method of reproduction.

....

.... **[2 marks]**

08.5 A gardener has been breeding roses in her garden.

She selects the roses with the biggest blossoms and most fragrant flowers to breed together, and pollinates them herself.

A farmer's cabbages suffer from white fly.

The farmer asks a local plant laboratory to create him a resistant breed of cabbage.

Describe the differences between the gardener's and the farmer's approaches to improving their plants.

[4 marks]

09.1 Explain the difference between **population size** and **population density**.

[2 marks]

09.2 Mr Green needs to assess the population of plantain on a 10 m wide path in a national park.

Figure 9.1 shows broadleaf plantain, which is a tough plant often found on footpaths.

Figure 9.1

Mr Green has a 25 cm² wire quadrat and a measuring tape.

He places the tape across the path, including the dense verges either side of the path.

What is the name of this line?

[1 mark]

09.3 Mr Green places the quadrat at the end of the line, in the verge.

He counts the number of whole plants in the quadrat and records the number.

How should Mr Green decide where to place the **next** quadrat along the line?

....

.... [2 marks]

09.4 Mr Green samples along the line, until he reaches the other end.

The whole path is 500 m long.

Describe the steps Mr Green should follow so that he has statistical evidence for the distribution of plantain **along the length of the path**.

....

....

.... [3 marks]

09.5 Explain why there are likely to be more plantains in the **middle** of the path than at the edges.

....

.... [2 marks]

END OF QUESTIONS

BLANK PAGE

Answers

Set A – Paper 1

Question	Answer(s)	Extra info	Mark(s)	AO/Spec ref.
01.1	Platelets — Forms clots to seal wounds; Skin — Acts as a barrier; Stomach — Produces acid to kill pathogens; Trachea and bronchi — Secretes mucus to trap pathogens all four correct for **3** marks two or three correct for **2** marks one correct for **1** mark		3	AO1 4.2.2.3 4.3.1.6
01.2	advantage: kill bacteria (inside body)	allow cures bacterial infection	1	AO1 4.3.1.8
	disadvantage: do not kill viruses	allow may lead to antibiotic resistant strains	1	
01.3	introduce dead / inactive / harmless / part of pathogens		1	4.3.1.7
	stimulates white blood cells to produce antibodies		1	
	in future if same pathogens re-enter the body, white blood cells produce antibodies very quickly		1	
	pathogens killed before can spread / cause symptoms		1	
02.1	60 mm = 60 000 μm		1	AO2 4.1.1.5
	actual size = image size ÷ magnification		1	
	= 60 000 ÷ 5000	allow 12 with no working shown for **4** marks allow equivalent marking points if conversion to μm is done at the end	1	
	= 12 (μm)		1	
02.2	resolution is the ability to distinguish between two points		1	AO1 4.1.1.5
	magnification is how many times bigger the image is than the object		1	
02.3	(not an animal) because it contains chloroplasts		1	AO2 4.1.1.1 4.1.1.2
	(not a plant) because it does not have a cell wall / it does not have a (large / permanent) vacuole		1	
	(not a bacterium) because it has a nucleus / has chloroplasts / does not have a cell wall / does not contain plasmids / does not have a naked loop of DNA		1	

Question	Answer(s)	Extra info	Mark(s)	AO/Spec ref.
03.1	**Level 3**: A coherent method is described with relevant detail, which demonstrates a broad understanding of the relevant scientific techniques and procedures. The steps in the method are logically ordered. The method would lead to the collection of valid results.		5-6	AO2/ AO3 4.2.2.1
	Level 2: The bulk of a method is described with mostly relevant detail, which demonstrates a reasonable understanding of the relevant techniques and procedures. The method may not be in a completely logical sequence and may be missing some detail.		3-4	
	Level 1: Discrete relevant points are made which demonstrate some understanding of the relevant scientific techniques and procedures. They may lack a logical structure and would not lead to the production of valid results.		1-2	
	No relevant content		0	
	Indicative content • independent variable is the temperature • temperature is varied by using different temperature water baths • dependent variable is time to digest all the starch • control variables include: concentration / amount of starch, pH • repeat readings and calculate means • plot graph of results to work out the optimum temperature that would give the shortest time / fastest rate of reaction			
03.2	protein — amino acids; lipid / fat / oil — glycerol and fatty acids		4	AO1 4.2.2.1
03.3	add Benedict's solution		1	AO1 4.2.2.1
	heat / put in a hot water bath		1	
	if sugar is present there is a colour change from blue to brick red / orange		1	
04.1	13 / at least 13		1	AO3 4.1.1.6
	each colony grew from one original bacterium		1	
04.2	it is a different species / type **or** there was contamination / imperfect aseptic technique		1	AO3 4.1.1.6

©HarperCollinsPublishers 2019

Biology Set A - Answers 87

Question	Answer(s)	Extra info	Mark(s)	AO/Spec ref.
04.3	any **two** from: • sterilise Petri dish • sterilise agar medium • sterilise inoculating loop • (when inoculating agar plate) only lift lid slightly • incubate upside down • ensure that the Petri dish is air tight apart from one very small section		2	**AO1** 4.1.1.6
04.4	radius (r) = 17.0 ÷ 2 = 8.5 (mm) area = 3.14 × 8.5² (mm²) = 227 (mm²) = 2.27 × 10² (mm²)	allow 2.27 × 10² with no working shown for **4 marks** deduct 1 mark if final answer not to 3 significant figures	1 1 1 1	**AO2** 4.1.1.6
04.5	take several measurements **and** take the mean / average		1	**AO2** 4.1.1.6
05.1	lack of leaves / chlorophyll means less photosynthesis so less glucose is made for growth / for making other substances necessary for growth		1 1 1	**AO2** 4.3.1.4 4.4.1.3
05.2	method 1: use fungicides explanation: these kill fungus / rose black spot method 2: remove / destroy infected leaves explanation: so they cannot act as a source of infection	explanation must be correctly linked to method it does **not** matter which is method 1 or method 2	1 1 1 1	**AO1/** **AO2** 4.3.1.4
06.1	lymphocytes can make antibodies (but not divide) tumour cells can divide (but not make antibodies) hybridoma cells can divide and make antibodies so produce many cells making monoclonal antibodies		1 1 1 1	**AO1** 4.3.2.1
06.2	antigens		1	**AO1** 4.3.2.1
06.3	monoclonal antibodies are joined to a toxic drug / radioactive substance which the monoclonal antibodies deliver to the cancer cells		1 1	**AO1** 4.3.2.2
06.4	only attach to the cancer cells do not harm other cells		1 1	**AO1** 4.3.2.2

Question	Answer(s)	Extra info	Mark(s)	AO/Spec ref.
07.1	% change = $\frac{\text{change} \times 100}{\text{original mass}}$ = $\frac{(29.0 - 24.0) \times 100}{24.0}$ = (+) 20.8 (%)	allow 20.8 with no working shown for **3 marks** deduct 1 mark for incorrect rounding	1 1 1	**AO2** 4.1.3.2
07.2	all points correctly plotted **2 marks** **but** three or four points correctly plotted **1 mark** smooth line of best fit	allow ± half a small square	2 1	**AO2** 4.1.3.2
07.3	correct reading from graph of where line crosses horizontal axis	allow ± half a small square	1	**AO3** 4.1.3.2
07.4	as one of the control variables surface area (:volume ratio) affects rate of osmosis		1 1	**AO2** 4.1.3.1 4.1.3.2
07.5	otherwise would include mass of solution in results / otherwise measurements of mass would be too high		1	**AO2** 4.1.3.2
08.1	phloem transports (dissolved) sugars		1	**AO2** 4.2.3.2
08.2	any **two** from: • phloem is made of elongated cells • xylem is made of hollow tubes • xylem contains lignin • phloem cells have companion cells next to them • phloem has small perforations / plasmodesmata / pores in the end walls		2	**AO1** 4.2.3.2
08.3	can find out how to treat them / get rid of them		1	**AO2** 4.3.3.1
08.4	(stomata close) to reduce water loss by transpiration / evaporation (disadvantage is) carbon dioxide cannot enter leaves so plant cannot photosynthesise		1 1 1 1	**AO2** 4.1.3.1 4.2.3.1 4.2.3.2 4.4.1.1
08.5	enters root hairs travels through xylem in transpiration stream / by transpiration		1 1 1	**AO2** 4.2.3.2
09.1	fatty material builds up inside coronary arteries reducing blood flow through coronary arteries / to heart muscle reducing supply of oxygen / glucose to heart muscle		1 1 1 1	**AO1** 4.2.2.4

Question	Answer(s)	Extra info	Mark(s)	AO/Spec ref.
09.2	**Level 3:** A detailed and coherent evaluation is provided which considers arguments on both sides as to whether the graph demonstrates that obesity is a risk factor for Type 2 diabetes, and comes to a conclusion consistent with the reasoning.		5-6	AO3 4.2.2.6
	Level 2: An attempt to give arguments on both sides as to whether the graph demonstrates that obesity is a risk factor for Type 2 diabetes. The logic may be inconsistent at times but builds towards a coherent argument.		3-4	
	Level 1: Discrete relevant points made. The logic may be unclear and the conclusion, if present, may not be consistent with the reasoning.		1-2	
	No relevant content		0	
	Indicative content • there does appear to be a link between body mass and Type 2 diabetes • but this could simply be correlation not causation • need more evidence, e.g. of a causal mechanism • not a perfect correlation • there may be other factors also linked with Type 2 diabetes • although graph shows body mass it does not show obesity • it's only over a 10-year period • we do not know where the data came from • we do not know how many people were involved			
10.1	**W:** the limiting factor is light intensity		1	AO2 4.4.1.2
	explanation: if you increase light intensity the rate of photosynthesis increases		1	
	X: the limiting factor is carbon dioxide concentration		1	
	explanation: if you increase carbon dioxide concentration the rate of photosynthesis increases		1	
	Y: the limiting factor is temperature		1	
	explanation: if you increase temperature the rate of photosynthesis increases		1	
10.2	**Level 3:** A detailed and coherent description of the tests that would have to be made and the conclusions that could be drawn depending on the outcomes.		5-6	AO2/ AO3 4.4.1.2

Question	Answer(s)	Extra info	Mark(s)	AO/Spec ref.
	Level 2: An attempt to give a description of the tests that would have to be made and the conclusions that could be drawn depending on the outcomes. The logic may be inconsistent at times but builds towards a coherent argument.		3-4	
	Level 1: Discrete relevant points made. The logic may be unclear and any conclusions, if present, may not be consistent with the reasoning.		1-2	
	No relevant content		0	
	Indicative content • limiting factor could be carbon dioxide concentration, temperature or amount of light • raise the temperature (above 25 °C) but leave carbon dioxide concentration (4%) the same • if the rate of photosynthesis increases then the limiting factor at **Z** is temperature • raise carbon dioxide concentration (above 4%) but leave the temperature (25 °C) the same • if the rate of photosynthesis increases then the limiting factor at **Z** is carbon dioxide concentration • if neither raising carbon dioxide concentration nor temperature increase the rate of photosynthesis then the limiting factor is light intensity			

Set A – Paper 2

Question	Answer(s)	Extra info	Mark(s)	AO/Spec ref.
01.1	amount of light		1	AO2 4.5.4.1
	place dishes in a box to keep light out		1	
	make sure light comes from all directions / dish is equally lit from all directions		1	
	because seedlings will also respond to the direction of light / seedlings are phototropic			
01.2	to make sure results are repeatable / to make sure result is not anomalous		1	AO2 4.5.4.1
01.3	auxin collected on lower side of shoot		1	AO2 4.5.4.1
	increased growth / elongation on lower side (causes upward growth)		1	
01.4	seedlings would grow horizontally		1	AO3 4.5.4.1
	auxin is evenly distributed / seedling experiences gravity on all parts equally because of rotation		1	
	so each side grows / elongates equally		1	

Question	Answer(s)	Extra info	Mark(s)	AO/Spec ref.
02.1	0		1	AO2 4.7.2.1
02.2	8		1	AO2 4.7.2.1
02.3	all points correctly plotted **3 marks** **but** at least 10 points correctly plotted **2 marks** **but** at least six points correctly plotted **1 mark** points joined up to make a 'kite'	allow ± half a small square	3 1	AO2 4.7.2.1
02.4	**Level 2:** A detailed and coherent argument is given, which explains why species B and D are more common on the path and why species A and C are more common away from the path.		3–4	AO3 4.7.1.1 4.7.2.1
	Level 1: Discrete relevant points are made, although the arguments may not be clear.		1–2	
	No relevant content		0	
	Indicative content <ul><li>species A and C are tall(er)</li><li>species A and C are killed by mowing on the path</li><li>species A and C can survive away from the path as they are tall enough to successfully compete for light</li><li>species B and D are low-growing</li><li>species B and D are not killed by mowing on the path / are missed by the mower</li><li>species B and D cannot survive away from the path as they are not tall enough to successfully compete for light</li></ul>			
03.1	**Level 3**: A coherent evaluation is given, with relevant details, which demonstrates an understanding of the principles of investigations and analysis of results.		5–6	AO3 4.5.2.1
	Level 2: An evaluation is given with mostly relevant detail, which demonstrates a reasonable understanding of the relevant principles. The evaluation may not be completely logical and may be missing some detail.		3–4	
	Level 1: Discrete relevant points are made which demonstrate some understanding of the relevant principles.		1–2	
	No relevant content		0	

Question	Answer(s)	Extra info	Mark(s)	AO/Spec ref.
	Indicative content **Method** <ul><li>only recording the shortest time for each student is not as representative as taking the mean result for each student</li><li>only using the right hand means that some students may not be using their dominant hand</li><li>different numbers of girls and boys is taken into account by taking mean results</li><li>sample sizes are small</li></ul> **Conclusion** <ul><li>it is correct that the mean time for the girls is less than for the boys</li><li>the results for the boys show more variation than for the girls</li><li>if the longest boys' result (0.32) is discounted then boys overall have the shortest reaction time</li><li>the conclusion is based on a small sample size</li><li>the conclusion should only apply to this way of measuring reaction time</li></ul>			
03.2	receptor = ear effector = hand muscles		1 1	AO2 4.5.2.1
03.3	electric impulses along neurones / nerve cells		1 1	AO1 4.5.2.1
03.4	no – no mark pressing the button is a conscious action **or** pressing the button is not an automatic action		1	AO2 4.5.2.1
04.1	<table><tr><th>Mitosis</th><th>Meiosis</th></tr><tr><td>✓</td><td>✗</td></tr><tr><td>✓</td><td>✗</td></tr><tr><td>✗</td><td>✓</td></tr><tr><td>✓</td><td>✗</td></tr></table> all correct for **2 marks** 4, 5, 6 or 7 correct for **1 mark**		2	AO1 4.6.1.1 4.6.1.2
04.2	sequence: 2, 3, 1, 4 all correct for **2 marks** 2 or 3 correct for **1 mark**		2	AO2 4.6.1.2
04.3	<table><tr><th></th><th>X</th><th>Y</th></tr><tr><td>X</td><td>XX female</td><td>XY male</td></tr><tr><td>X</td><td>XX female</td><td>XY male</td></tr></table> correct gametes correct offspring genotypes correct identification of female offspring correct probability of 0.5 **or** 50% **or** 1 in 2 **or** ½		1 1 1 1	AO1 4.6.1.6 4.6.1.8

Question	Answer(s)	Extra info	Mark(s)	AO/Spec ref.
04.4	0.5 or 50% or 1 in 2 or ½		1	AO2 4.6.1.6 4.6.1.8
05.1	to stimulate egg maturation / development		1	AO1 4.6.1.6
05.2	in a laboratory / in a dish		1	AO1 4.5.3.6
05.3	(reason:) success rates are low to increase chance of success (disadvantage:) multiple pregnancy / birth risk to mother / babies		1 1 1 1	AO1 4.5.3.5
05.4	FSH = X LH = W oestrogen = Z progesterone = Y all correct for **3** marks 2 or 3 correct for **2** marks 1 correct for **1** mark		3	AO1 4.5.3.4
06.1	decreases / goes down ADH / antidiuretic hormone decreases / goes down increases / goes up	in this order only	1 1 1 1	AO1 4.5.3.3
06.2	the idea that a change in one direction brings about a change in the opposite direction		1	AO1 4.5.3.3
06.3	to remove urea		1	AO1 4.5.3.3
07.1	Y = sugar Z = phosphate		1 1	AO1 4.6.1.5
07.2	nucleotide		1	AO1 4.6.1.5
07.3	it is made up of repeating units / nucleotides		1	AO1 4.6.1.5
07.4	TAAGCGAGT all correct for **2** marks at least half correct for **1** mark		2	AO1 4.6.1.5
07.5	three		1	AO2 4.6.1.5
08.1	Dd	allow dD	1	AO2 4.6.1.6 4.6.1.7
08.2	DD		1	AO2 4.6.1.6 4.6.1.7
08.3	does not have polydactyly	allow normal	1	AO2 4.6.1.6 4.6.1.7

Question	Answer(s)	Extra info	Mark(s)	AO/Spec ref.
08.4	no – no mark parents must both be dd child needs to inherit at least one D to have condition		1 1	AO2 4.6.1.6 4.6.1.7
08.5	**Level 2:** A detailed and coherent argument is given, which states all possible genotypes for A and C, and fully explains the reasoning leading to the conclusions.		3–4	AO2 4.6.1.6 4.6.1.7
	Level 1: Discrete relevant points are made, including some of the possible genotypes, although the reasoning may not be clear.		1–2	
	No relevant content		0	
	Indicative content **A:** • A = Dd or DD • A has condition so must have at least one D • but not enough information to tell whether A is Dd or DD **C:** • C = Dd • C has condition so must have at least one D • C has a mother (B) who must be dd, so C must have inherited a d from B **or** • C has a child (F) who must be dd, so C must have passed on a d to F			
08.6	if disorder is caused by a dominant allele then each individual carrying the allele is affected by the disorder **or** if disorder is caused by a recessive allele then heterozygous individuals can carry and pass on the condition even though they are unaffected		1	AO2 4.6.1.7
09.1	variation in size among wrens / some wrens were larger than others variation in size is affected / controlled by different genes larger wrens are more likely to survive / live longer than smaller ones larger wrens pass on the genes for being larger / genes for being smaller are not passed on		1 1 1 1	AO2 4.6.2.1 4.6.2.2
09.2	breed them together to produce fertile offspring		1 1	AO2 4.6.2.2

©HarperCollins*Publishers* 2019   Biology Set A - Answers   **91**

Question	Answer(s)	Extra info	Mark(s)	AO/Spec ref.
09.3	first two names / genus and species name are the same because they are the same species		1	AO3 4.6.4
	the different / third name shows that there is a difference		1	
09.4	*Troglodytes hirtensis*		1	AO2 4.6.4
	same genus name because similar, but different species name		1	
10.1	**Level 3**: A detailed and coherent explanation is given, with relevant details, which demonstrates an understanding of the efficiency of biomass transfer along food chains and its implications for the future feeding of the human population.		5–6	AO1/ AO2/ AO3 4.7.4.3
	Level 2: A description and explanation is given with mostly relevant detail, which demonstrates a reasonable understanding of the relevant principles. The argument may not be completely logical and may be missing some detail.		3–4	
	Level 1: Discrete relevant points are made which demonstrate some understanding of the relevant principles.		1–2	
	No relevant content		0	
	Indicative content • biomass / energy is lost between trophic levels • only about 10% (on average) of the biomass / energy from one trophic level is transferred to the next • some biomass / energy is lost from food chains because not all ingested materials are absorbed / some are egested as faeces • some biomass / energy is lost from food chains because some is lost as waste such as carbon dioxide / urea • some biomass / energy is lost from food chains because large amounts of glucose are used in respiration • more biomass / energy is available to humans by eating at a lower trophic level • there is more food available / more people can be fed, if they eat at a lower trophic level • as the human population increases / food becomes more scarce, people will need to eat more plant crops and less meat			
10.2	less energy / biomass is used in respiration		1	AO2 4.7.4.3
	more energy / biomass is passed to next trophic level		1	

Question	Answer(s)	Extra info	Mark(s)	AO/Spec ref.
11.1	**Level 3**: A coherent description and explanation is given, with relevant details, which demonstrates an understanding of the links between predator and prey populations.		5–6	AO3 4.7.2.1
	Level 2: A description and explanation is given with mostly relevant detail, which demonstrates a reasonable understanding of the relevant principles. The argument may not be completely logical and may be missing some detail.		3–4	
	Level 1: Discrete relevant points are made which demonstrate some understanding of the relevant principles.		1–2	
	No relevant content		0	
	Indicative content • snowy owls nest when there are peaks in lemming abundance • snowy owls do not nest when lemming abundance is low • this is because snowy owls need lemmings to feed their young / they could not raise young if there were not enough lemmings to eat • lemming abundance falls after the years when snowy owls have nested • this is because so many lemmings have been eaten by the snowy owls and their young • lemming numbers begin to rise in the years after snowy owls have nested • this is because there is less predation as there will be fewer snowy owls • there is not a perfect correlation between snowy owl nesting and lemming abundance • for example, the years with the highest number of nests are not the years with the highest lemming abundance • this may be because snowy owls may be forced to breed on the island as they are less able to breed elsewhere			
11.2	respiration by snowy owls		1	AO1 4.7.2.2
	decay of waste / dead bodies		1	
	respiration by microorganisms (responsible for decay)		1	
11.3	by protecting places with a higher biodiversity more species may be protected		1	AO3 4.7.3.1
	places with a low biodiversity have their own unique species which should also be protected		1	

Set B – Paper 1

Question	Answer(s)	Extra info	Mark(s)	AO/Spec ref.
01.2	poison		1	AO1 4.3.3.2
01.2	any **two** of: • thorns and hairs to **deter animals** • specialised leaves **which droop or curl when touched** • mimicry to **trick animals**	must include action of how defence works (in bold) do not accept bark, cellulose cell walls, waxy cuticle do not award 3 marks for 3 defences, action of defence must be linked to the defence mechanism	2 + 2	AO1 4.3.3.2
01.3	any **two** of: • skin • mucus • hairs in nose • trachea / bronchi • stomach acid • tears	accept any other reasonable answer	2	AO1 4.3.1.6
01.4	any **two** of: • phagocytosis • antibody production • antitoxin production (allow descriptions instead)		2	AO1 4.3.1.6
02.1	tobacco mosaic virus	allow other viral disease, if correct	1	AO1 4.3.1.2
02.2	it gives a distinctive 'mosaic' pattern of discolouration on the leaves, which affects the growth of the plant due to lack of photosynthesis	allow other correct answers related to student's answer above	1 1 1	AO1 4.3.1.2
02.3	black spot	allow other fungal disease, if correct	1	AO1 4.3.1.4
02.4	either: stunted growth caused by nitrate deficiency because nitrate ions needed for protein synthesis and therefore growth **or** chlorosis caused by magnesium deficiency because magnesium ions needed to make chlorophyll	name of correct ion must be stated – 1 related effect – 1 related reason – 1	3	AO1 4.3.3.1

Question	Answer(s)	Extra info	Mark(s)	AO/Spec ref.
03.1	enzymes		1	AO1 4.2.2.1
03.2	proteases break down **proteins** to **amino acids** lipases break down **lipids** to glycerol and **fatty acids**	accept fats (instead of lipids)	1 1 1 1	AO1 4.2.2.1
03.3	amylase, buffer, starch	must be correct order	1	AO2 4.2.2.1
03.4	buffer must be added to the enzyme before the starch is added – as the reaction will start as soon as the enzyme and starch meet if no buffer (or added afterwards) results will not be valid as the pH will be changed after the reaction has started		1 1	AO2 4.2.2.1
03.5	iodine plus a drop of water		1	AO2 4.2.2.1
03.6	a control makes it easier to compare colours as the water in the control doesn't contain any starch / so you can be sure all the starch is gone / digested / broken down, if it is the same colour as the control		1 1	AO2 4.2.2.1
04.1	virus bacterium red blood cell leaf cell	**all** must be in correct order for mark	1	AO1 4.1.1.1 4.1.1.2
04.2	to keep specimen flat to retain liquid under it to prevent specimen drying out	allow – to prevent the specimen touching the microscope lens	1 1	AO1 4.1.1.2
04.3	smaller field of view with a high-power lens **because** has greater magnification	or converse: larger with low power lens because smaller magnification. must state reason (i.e. *because*... for 2 marks, not just high is smaller and low is bigger)	1 1	AO1 4.1.1.2 4.1.1.5
04.4	iodine solution		1	AO1 4.1.1.2

©HarperCollins*Publishers* 2019

Biology Set B - Answers 93

Question	Answer(s)	Extra info	Mark(s)	AO/Spec ref.
04.5	(diagram showing Region of elongation, Meristem – region of cell division, Root cap) Scale bar should be approximately 10 mm long and labelled 2 mm	1 mark for drawing, with distinct meristem area. Must state meristem, not just region of cell division 1 mark for label 1 mark for sensible units / scale 1 mark for correct scale bar	2 2	AO2 4.2.3.1 4.1.1.2
04.6	meristem tissue can differentiate into any type of plant cell, throughout life of plant		1	AO1 4.1.2.3
05.1	accept values in range 65 000–70 000		1	AO2 4.2.2.5 4.2.2.6
05.2	active = nearly 4000 incidences (allow ± 1000) drink less alcohol = 12 000 incidences (allow ± 1000) and therefore drinking less alcohol produced about three times fewer cancers as being active	1 mark for both readings must include the comparison for 2nd mark	1 1	AO2 4.2.2.5 4.2.2.6
05.3	eat fruit and veg lots of fibre low salt low processed / red meat low alcohol	must include low alcohol for 2 marks (to reward recognising alcohol / drinks are part of the diet) and at least two others	2	AO2 4.2.2.6 4.2.2.7
05.4	men and women make different lifestyle choices men and women are exposed to different environmental factors men and women have structural and genetic differences		1 1 1	AO3 4.2.2.5 4.2.2.6 4.2.2.7

Question	Answer(s)	Extra info	Mark(s)	AO/Spec ref.
06.1	lymphocytes detect antigens on dead / inactive Lumpius and produce specific antibodies against Lumpius / pathogen antibodies lock onto Lumpius	accept white blood cells instead of lymphocytes	2	AO2 4.3.1.6 4.3.1.7
06.2	lymphocytes remember the shape of the antigen	accept white blood cells instead of lymphocytes	1	AO2 4.3.1.6 4.3.1.7
06.3	lymphocytes instantly recognise live Lumpius / pathogen because it has the same antigens as the vaccine and respond **more quickly** to the infection by producing many specific antibodies, which lock onto the Lumpius / pathogen and kill them before person becomes ill / person is immune / has immunity	accept white blood cells instead of lymphocytes must state 'more quickly' or equivalent and must express concept that person does not become ill	3	AO2 4.3.1.6 4.3.1.7
06.4	efficacy – vaccine works / looks promising / passes to next stage of trial / positive result **because** many specific antibodies are produced when volunteers are infected with live Lumpius / pathogen dose – is good / correct **because** response elicited (i.e. production of antibodies).	must give reason for answers accept caution – insufficient data, adverse side effects / deaths – is dose too high? Can acknowledge this thought process	1 1 1 1	AO3 4.3.1.9
06.5	clinical trial many volunteers recruited / tested on many humans		1 1	AO3 4.3.1.9
07.1	oxygen		1	AO1 4.4.1.2
07.2	a clock / watch a ruler / other measuring device	allow thermometer, if its use is explained below	2	AO2 4.4.1.2

94 Biology Set B - Answers

Question	Answer(s)	Extra info	Mark(s)	AO/Spec ref.
07.3	**Level 3:** A detailed and coherent explanation is provided with most of the relevant content, which demonstrates a comprehensive understanding of the investigation and the order in which it is carried out. The response gives logical steps, with reasons.		5–6	**AO2** 4.4.1.2
	Level 2: A detailed and coherent explanation is provided. The student has a broad understanding of the investigation. The response makes mainly logical steps with some reasoning.		3–4	
	Level 1: Simple descriptions of the investigation are made along with reference to photosynthesis. The response demonstrates limited logical linking of points.		1–2	
	No relevant content		0	
	Indicative content • set up apparatus as in diagram • make sure plant photosynthesising (can see bubbles of oxygen) • measure and record the temperature of water in beaker; the water is intended to maintain a constant temperature (buffer), so the temperature should be taken periodically and kept constant; controlling other variables • measure and place lamp a specified distance from apparatus – control of light intensity related to distance of lamp from apparatus • carry out at several different distances of lamp (five distances) • allow plant to acclimatise to each new distance of the lamp / light intensity (2 mins) • record production rate of oxygen – count bubbles over given time period – 1 min / 5 mins, at each distance • repeat three times for each distance of the lamp / light intensity • calculate mean production oxygen rate • light intensity not linearly related to distance			
07.4	use a graduated syringe or measuring cylinder to collect the gas / oxygen		1	**AO3** 4.4.1.2
07.5	lots of sunshine = lots of oxygen produced / high rate of photosynthesis and therefore lots of oxygen good for fish in pond	allow converse lack of sunshine / in shady area = lower rate of photosynthesis / less oxygen produced allow converse in shade = not so good for fish	1 1	**AO3** 4.4.1.2

Question	Answer(s)	Extra info	Mark(s)	AO/Spec ref.
07.6	inverse square law / inverse proportion		1	**AO3** 4.4.1.2
	as light intensity increases (distance between lamp and plant decreases) the volume of oxygen (or the rate of bubble production) increases.	allow converse	1	
	this indicates the rate of photosynthesis increases with light intensity	allow converse	1	
08.1	there is incomplete oxidation of glucose		1	**AO1** 4.4.2.1 4.4.2.2
08.2	[graph with labels A (EPOC), B (steady-state O₂ consumption), C (O₂ requirement), D (end exercise), E (end recovery)]	recovery label can be indicated anywhere in the shaded EPOC area labels can be either on the graph shape, or correctly placed on the x and y axes	5	**AO2** 4.4.2.1 4.4.2.2
08.3	blood flowing through the muscles transports the lactic acid to the **liver** where it is **converted** back **into glucose**		1 1	**AO1** 4.4.2.1 4.4.2.2
08.4	oxygen debt is the amount of **extra** oxygen the body needs (compared with resting) **after** exercise to react with the accumulated lactic acid / remove it from the cells.	must convey idea of **extra** oxygen	1 1	**AO1** 4.4.2.1 4.4.2.2
08.5	person B		1	**AO3** 4.4.2.2
08.6	any **two** of: for person B: • heart rate increases more slowly / doesn't increase as fast • heart rate reaches a lower steady state • decreases more quickly after exercise / recovers more quickly / returns to resting rate quicker	allow converse for person A allow reaches a lower maximum allow converse for person A allow converse for person A Must be clear which person is being referred to	2	**AO3** 4.4.2.2

©HarperCollins*Publishers* 2019 — Biology Set B – Answers — 95

Question	Answer(s)	Extra info	Mark(s)	AO/Spec ref.
09.1	Substances are moved across a cell membrane from a more dilute solution to a more concentrated solution (against a concentration gradient).		2	**AO1** 4.1.3.3
09.2	Any **one** from: • Chemical reactions to synthesise / produce / new / larger molecules • Movement • Keeping warm		1	**AO1** 4.4.2.1
09.3	**Level 3:** A detailed and coherent description is provided with most of the relevant content, which demonstrates a comprehensive understanding of metabolism and how living processes are linked. The response is logical		5–6	**AO1** 4.1.3.1 4.2.2.1
	Level 2: A detailed and coherent description is provided. The student has a broad understanding of metabolism. The response makes mainly logical steps with some linkage.		3–4	4.4.1.3 4.4.2.1
	Level 1: Simple descriptions of living processes are made. The response demonstrates limited logical linking of points.		1–2	4.4.2.3
	No relevant content		0	
	Indicative content • conversion of glucose to starch, glycogen and cellulose • the formation of lipid molecules from a molecule of glycerol and three molecules of fatty acids • the use of glucose and nitrate ions to form amino acids which in turn are used to synthesise proteins • breakdown of excess proteins to form urea for excretion. • uses of glucose produced in photosynthesis - respiration, storage, to produce fat or oil for storage, to strengthen the cell wall • used to produce amino acids for protein synthesis.			
10.1	reduce / stop water loss / rehydration		1	**AO1** 4.2.3.2
	by reducing (rate of) transpiration		1	
10.2	reduce / stop oxygen uptake so reducing (rate of) respiration	reduce / stop carbon dioxide uptake so reducing (rate of) photosynthesis	1 1	**AO3** 4.2.3.2 4.4.1.1 4.4.2.1

Set B – Paper 2

Question	Answer(s)	Extra info	Mark(s)	AO/Spec ref.
01.1	abiotic		1	**AO 1** 4.7.1.1
01.2	any two from: • light • space • water • mineral ions	do not accept food	2	**AO 1** 4.7.1.1
01.3	any two from: • food • territory • water	do not accept space	2	**AO 1** 4.7.1.1
01.4	interdependence		1	**AO 1** 4.7.1.1
01.5	a community in which all the species and environmental factors are in balance		1	**AO 1** 4.7.1.1
	so that population sizes remain fairly constant		1	
01.6	methane		1	**AO1** 4.7.2.3
01.7	mineral ions		1	**AO1** 4.7.2.2
02.1	nervous system: • fast acting • acts for short time • acts in a specific area • electrical hormonal system: • slow acting • acts for long time • acts more generally • chemical		2 2	**AO1** 4.5.2.1 4.5.3.1
02.2	84 × 4 = 336 336 – 85 – 87 – 83 = 81 ms	must state units for third mark	1 1 1	**AO3** 4.5.2.1
02.3	as more alcohol is consumed, reaction times increase, e.g. with 0.5 units / half a can, mean reaction time is 33 ms, increasing to 84 ms with 6 units / cans of beer	reference must be made to figures / results for second mark, as candidates asked to use the results	2	**AO3** 4.5.2.1
02.4	2000 people used as part of the study, increases repeatability (in second study) / too few volunteers (in first study)		1	**AO3** 4.5.2.1
	lack of repeats in first study = less repeatable		1	

Question	Answer(s)	Extra info	Mark(s)	AO/Spec ref.
03.1	sensible scales on correct axis		1	AO3 4.5.3.2
	correctly plotting points		1	
	drawing line – joining points or line of best fit		1	
	labels on axis –y axis – percentage of population who have Type 2 diabetes (%), and x axis – mean body mass (kg)		1	
03.2	correlation / positive correlation, as mean body mass increases so does percentage / incidence of type 2 diabetes		1	AO3 4.5.3.2
03.3	**Level 3:** A detailed and coherent explanation is provided with most of the relevant content, which demonstrates a comprehensive understanding of the negative feedback system and how blood glucose concentrations differ in people with and without diabetes after a meal. The response gives logical steps, with reasons.		5-6	AO1 4.5.3.2 4.5.3.7
	Level 2: A detailed and coherent explanation is provided. The student has a broad understanding of the negative feedback system and diabetes. The response makes mainly logical steps with some reasoning.		3-4	
	Level 1: Simple description of diabetes is made along with reference to the negative feedback system. The response demonstrates limited logical linking of points.		1-2	
	No relevant content		0	
	Indicative content • (in both people) glucose levels detected by pancreas • and stimulated to release insulin in to blood • also release of glucagon is suppressed • insulin binds with receptors on cells • cells take up glucose • there are fewer of these receptors in the diabetic person • glucose is converted into glycogen in cells • and so levels in blood are reduced • after breakfast the concentrations of blood glucose increase, in both people • but person with diabetes increases **much more** • both their concentrations decrease during the morning, but person with diabetes decreases much more slowly			

Question	Answer(s)	Extra info	Mark(s)	AO/Spec ref.
04.1	zebrafish		1	AO3 4.6.4
04.2	fugu and green spotted puffer		1	AO3 4.6.4
04.3	167.7 million years ago	must give units accept mya	1	AO3 4.6.4
04.4	insufficient evidence currently to be more accurate		1	AO3 4.6.3.2 4.6.4
04.5	either: fossils or DNA profiling or antibiotic resistance (in case of bacteria)		1	AO1 4.6.3.4 4.6.3.5
04.6	**Level 3:** A detailed and coherent explanation is provided with most of the relevant content, which demonstrates a comprehensive understanding of speciation and how medaka and stickleback may have become separate species. The response gives logical steps, with reasons.		5-6	AO2 4.6.2.1 4.6.2.2 4.6.3.1 4.6.3.2
	Level 2: A detailed and coherent explanation is provided. The student has a broad understanding of speciation and refers to medaka and stickleback. The response makes mainly logical steps with some reasoning.		3-4	
	Level 1: Simple descriptions of speciation are made along with reference to the medaka and stickleback. The response demonstrates limited logical linking of points.		1-2	
	No relevant content		0	
	Indicative content • definition of species as organisms that are able to interbreed to produce fertile offspring • barriers separate ancestral species so they are no longer able to breed • most commonly physical / geological, can also be reproductive or ecological; examples given should be in relation to fish, e.g. river split course, courtship behaviour, changes in pH or salinity • 96-150 mya stickleback and medaka had a common ancestor that was a different species from either of them • this fish species got separated into two groups • random mutations occur in each isolated group of fish / different mutations in each group • the fish best suited to the environment survive and pass on their genes			

Question	Answer(s)	Extra info	Mark(s)	AO/Spec ref.
	• if the environment is different, for each group of fish, selection pressure means that different mutations are favoured by natural selection • over a long period of time • different characteristics will develop in the different fish groups • if the barrier were removed / the fish were able to mix again, they would no longer be able to breed and so are considered separate species			
05.1	cerebral cortex		1	AO1 4.5.2.2
05.2	cerebellum		1	AO1 4.5.2.2
05.3	medulla		1	AO1 4.5.2.2
05.4	A – coordination of complex functions, e.g. learning, memory, emotions and conscious thought B – unconscious / automatic functions, e.g. movement and balance C – unconscious / automatic (and homeostatic), e.g. swallowing, digestion and vomiting, breathing and heart rate	allow specific example of complex function 1 for general function plus second mark for example, for each area	2 2 2	AO2 4.5.2.2
05.5	strong positive correlation / as animal increases in weight so does the size of their brain not directly proportional / body weight increases a lot for a smaller increase in brain / any other comment about the relationship consistent with the graph		1 1	AO3 4.5.1 4.5.2.1
05.6	either: • a larger animal requires a bigger brain to control / coordinate its living processes or • metabolism of animal / energy demands of brain limits brain size so if the animal is larger it is able to support the energy requirements of a larger brain		1	AO2 4.5.1 4.5.2.1
05.7	other factors have more effect, e.g. evolution and ecological niche occupied		1	AO2 4.5.1 4.5.2.1
06.1	thymine		1	AO1 4.6.1.5
06.2	3		1	AO1 4.6.1.5

Question	Answer(s)	Extra info	Mark(s)	AO/Spec ref.
06.3	**Level 3:** A detailed and coherent explanation is provided with most of the relevant content, which demonstrates a comprehensive understanding of protein synthesis and how it may be disrupted in Leigh syndrome. The response gives logical steps, with reasons.		5-6	AO2 4.6.1.5
	Level 2: A detailed and coherent explanation is provided. The student has a broad understanding of protein synthesis and that errors can cause the wrong protein to be made. The response makes mainly logical steps with some reasoning.		3-4	
	Level 1: Simple descriptions of protein synthesis are made along with reference to errors. The response demonstrates limited logical linking of points.		1-2	
	No relevant content		0	
	Indicative content • proteins consist of chains of amino acids, coded for by a triplet of bases • each protein has a particular number and sequence of amino acids • if this is altered, then the wrong protein is made • transcription happens in the cell nucleus where the DNA is copied • the two DNA strands unzip, complementary bases pair up with bases on the template strand • C pairs with G, U pairs with A to form a strand of mRNA, which travels to the ribosome, where it is translated • the ribosome reads off the triplet codes and carrier molecules bring specific amino acids to the protein chain in the correct order • the amino acids bond together to form a polypeptide chain, which folds to a specific shape to form a protein • Leigh syndrome could be a problem with unzipping, or a problem with transcription – the wrong base pairs with the template strand. Or the ribosome may read the codon incorrectly or the carrier molecule brings the wrong amino acid. All of which would cause the wrong protein to be made.			

Question	Answer(s)	Extra info	Mark(s)	AO/Spec ref.
06.4	any two from: • search for genes linked to different types of disease • understanding and treatment of inherited disorders • use in tracing human migration patterns from the past	allow specific correct examples	2	AO1 4.6.1.4
07.1	any one from: • green plants • algae / weed • producers / primary producers		1	AO2 4.7.2.1 4.7.4.1
07.2	*T. sarasinorum* numbers increase and they eat lots of fish eggs therefore fewer fish survive from the eggs and there are fewer to eat, so 'elongated' eats more shrimp 'thicklip' numbers decrease as they are now in direct competition for shrimp, not enough shrimp for all		1 1 1	AO2 4.7.1.1 4.7.1.3 4.7.2.1
07.3	live in different habitats (1 mark only) *T. opudi* lives in bush cover and rocks, whereas *T. wahjui* lives on the muddy bottom		1 1	AO2 4.7.1.1 4.7.2.1
07.4	any one from: • sewage • fertiliser run-off • toxic chemicals		1	AO1 4.7.3.2
07.5	energy (/stored in biomass) is lost at each stage through waste products, respiration, movement and maintaining a constant body temperature therefore there is insufficient energy to maintain another population at the top		1 1 1	AO1 4.7.4.2 4.7.4.3
08.1	A – nucleus containing DNA removed from egg cell B – electric pulse causes skin cell to fuse with egg cell C – cell fusion D – cell division E – (early-stage) embryo is implanted into surrogate		5	AO2 4.6.2.5
08.2	variation		1	AO2 4.6.2.1
08.3	any two from: plants that reproduce with tubers or runners (1 mark each) bacteria aphids / insects that reproduce asexually any other valid example	accept specific plants, e.g. potatoes, strawberries	2	AO1 4.6.1.1

Question	Answer(s)	Extra info	Mark(s)	AO/Spec ref.
08.4	any two from: • only one parent needed • more time and energy efficient as do not need to find a mate • faster than sexual reproduction • many identical offspring can be produced when conditions are favourable • genetically identical, so if parent is well adapted to environment offspring will be too		2	AO1 4.6.1.3
08.5	the gardener's method: • involves **selective breeding** • is the traditional method of breeding together individuals with desired characteristics • is the more natural method • takes a long time (many generations) • offspring won't definitely have trait the gardener wants the farmer's method: • involves **genetic engineering** • is more technical • is faster by transplanting specific genes for desired characteristics • is more expensive • offspring will definitely have the desired traits		2 (two points required) 2 (two points required)	AO2 4.6.2.3 4.6.2.4
09.1	population size means the number of individuals of a species that live in a habitat (number) population density is the number of individuals in a given / specific area		1 1	AO1 4.7.1.1
09.2	transect		1	AO2 4.7.1.1
09.3	systematic sampling: at regular intervals (e.g. every 50 cm) intervals must be sufficient to capture the changes in vegetative cover		1 1	AO2 4.7.1.1
09.4	construct further transects at 10 m intervals / other sensible distance down the path take quadrats at the same distances as before (as suggested in Q09.3) along these transects calculate the means at each quadrat place along the length of the path (add up all the plantains and divide by number of quadrats along the length of the path) to give mean number across the path		1 1 1	AO2 4.7.1.1
09.5	plants complete with each other for limited resources / many plants at verge, lots of competition plantain leaves are tough / have adapted to being trampled and may out complete more delicate plants, which are trampled in the middle of the path		1 1	AO3 4.7.1 4.7.1.3 4.7.1.4

BLANK PAGE

BLANK PAGE

BLANK PAGE

BLANK PAGE